Alignment

God's Will or Mine

Alignment
God's Will or Mine

An in-depth study of the book of James

Moriah J. Hagel

Carpenter's Son Publishing

Published by Carpenter's Son Publishing, Franklin, Tennessee
www.carpenterssonpublishing.com

Scripture quotations are taken from The New King James Version (NKJV) /
Thomas Nelson Publishers, Nashville: Thomas Nelson Publishers.,
Copyright © 1982. Used by permission. All rights reserved.

Edited by Ann Tatlock

Cover and Interior Design by Suzanne Lawing

978-1-956370-05-8

Printed in the United States of America

Jesus, this book is to You for Your Glory. Please use it to encourage Your children in their walk with You.

Contents

Acknowledgments

Always a thank you to Jesus first. Thank You, Lord, for Your wisdom that You taught me as we walked through the book of James together. You have been faithful every step of the way.

Thank you to Mom and Dad who read over this manuscript before I sent it to be edited. You both have been an example of endurance, mercy and grace that I cannot find anywhere else. Thank you for running this race of life before me and with me. Keep running hard, because I am watching to gain wisdom on how to do this. Thank you also to Ann Tatlock for your edits and guidance.

Preface

Dear Reader,

According to my support and editing team, these devotionals are a little heavy. Therefore, I recommend this book for older, more established Christians. If you are new to the faith, and still want to read and go through this book with me, I suggest you find an established Christian of the same gender to walk through this with you. If you are wondering why I chose the verses to focus on that I did, it is because I walked through this with Jesus myself and these were the verses He brought to my attention. This is a study that is personal to me because it comes out of a time when the Lord and I walked through difficult trials in my life. I was feeling foolish, worn out from spiritual battles raging in my life, defeated, and gullible to the tricks of the enemy. My struggles included a desired romantic relationship that ended, as well as my concern for a friend who was walking down a dangerous path. At the same time my world was turned upside down in a painful way when the pandemic shut down church and Bible studies and the annual conference in which I played a major part. God, in His mercy, would guide me to the concepts I needed at that time to teach me how to better prepare for the battles to come. He taught me so much, and I wanted to share His lessons with you. Welcome aboard and may God complete the work He has begun in you.

A common misunderstanding among twenty-first century Christians has to do with the trials in our lives and the battle that rages around us. We too often view these as punishments when that isn't necessarily so. Paul tells us there is a war between our soul and flesh. We know who wins in the end, but the question is, will we fight to be on Christ's side everyday of our lives? I began studying the book of James at the beginning of 2020. As for most of us, it was for me a year full of trials that would test my faith. While going through it, God told me I was "fighting for my soul." James' words convicted me and reestablished within me what I believed and how I should walk in total alignment with Christ. Am I there yet after God walked me through the lessons in this book? No, but I am closer than I was. My hope is that this study does the same for you and sharpens your weapons for the war ahead so we can stand with Christ together. So grab a journal and let's study together.

DAY ONE

Alignment as a Bondservant

"James, a bondservant of God and of the Lord Jesus Christ, to the twelve tribes which are scattered abroad: Greetings."
James 1:1

One year my family went to a camp as a retreat. At that camp there was this one boy, probably ten years old, who was the most annoying kid that whole weekend. For one of the activities we had the choice to go horseback riding. Well, when this individual got there the horse guides explained to him that there were only so many horses and he had to wait his turn. I don't remember a whole lot from that camp, but I do remember his response. He said, "I don't want to argue with you, I just want to say...." His whole mindset was not on listening, nor on obeying the rules; it was on getting what he wanted. He was not honoring anyone and certainly, at that time, did not have the mindset that James has here, as a bondservant.

Many of the early church fathers described themselves as bondservants. A bondservant was a slave who at their time of freedom chose to remain a slave because their master was good. They chose to forever follow Christ and make Him the ruler and master of their lives. For them, it was a choice to follow God's will for their life. Many of us have taken the step of accepting Christ as our Savior, but choosing the life of a bondservant is the next step. It is like that ten-year-old. He had come to camp, but he was not respecting the words of the staff. When we are first "saved" we want to please God, but sometimes as we get older in our Christianity we don't try as hard. Where are we in our relationship with Christ? Will we obey as if He is our master or are we at a place of negotiation with Him? "I don't want to argue, I just want to say ..." The first church in Revelation was guilty of losing their first love. Are we? Does it no longer bring joy to us to obey God? Are we out of the honeymoon stage? We don't have to get there. My parents are still in the honeymoon stage and they have been married over forty years. Now it does take work to stay there, but it is work we should be willing to do.

A bondservant chose their lifestyle because they had seen their master be good and faithful, and they would trust him to continue to be that way; therefore, they submitted themselves under his authority for the rest of their lives, and then to the son's authority as well. If we watch God, we will find Him faithful. We see this all throughout the Old and New Testament. David said, "I am old and I have never seen the righteous forsaken or their descendants begging for bread."[1] We all know that person who, whenever hardship comes, does not expect God to provide what is needed. Sometimes we are

---

1. Psalm 37:25

that one. Why do we think His goodness and faithfulness ends? Because of that fear, we don't make ourselves devoted followers of Christ. Is it because we do not truly know Him?

When I was little we barely had enough money to get by. But those are some of the happiest times Mom and Dad remember because God was providing what we needed. At that time in our lives there were six of us kids, and since we were hitting our growth spurts we needed blue jeans. Mom and Dad told us to pray, and God sent boxes of blue jeans. Dad, as a northerner, was craving rhubarb, and God provided a whole case. Another example is for Christmas our gift was a healthy little brother, but God sent more. Through God using our church, our couch was full of new sweaters and dolls for each of us. My older sister still has her doll from that Christmas. These are just some of the provisions God gave us during that time. Mom and Dad had to rely on Christ and Christ alone. If Dad had thought God inadequate and had not obeyed Him when He said to get out of the military, get out of debt and trust Him, we would have never seen heaven's flood gates open the way they did. God is the same yesterday, today and forever.[2] He is faithful to all generations.[3] Will we devote our lives to God, as bondservants, no matter what? Yes, there are times when it looks like we are failing, but are we obeying? Are we being a bondservant of God and of the Lord Jesus Christ?

There will also be times when we are alone, but be of good cheer, you are never the only one walking this path and you are never walking where the Master is not if we walk in obedi-

---

2. Hebrews 13:8

3. Psalm 119:90

ence. That is the reason James wrote this epistle, to encourage the scattered Christians. Even when Elijah felt that he was the only prophet left in all of Israel, God was hiding one hundred other prophets through one faithful servant.[4] Being a bond-servant can be hard, but we are not alone, and our God who is faithful and good has a reward for us in the end.

APPLICATION:

In what areas of your life have you lost your first love and are not living as a bondservant to Christ? Look at one area of your life that needs to be brought into alignment with Christ and write down a battle plan with practical steps to getting back in step with Christ in that area. Begin today to implement your plan. May you fight your flesh well and be victorious!

---

4. 1 Kings 18:4

Alignment Through Joy

"My brethren, count it all joy when you fall into various trials, knowing that the testing of your faith produces patience."
James 1:2-3

My sisters drive Priuses, and they like to test them and see just how far they can go before filling up with gas. Because of this experience, when their tanks ding empty, they have peace and know just how far they can still go before having to actually fill up. Similarly, life is our testing period. When we come out victoriously we know how far God can take us and that we can endure through Christ who strengthens us. Our neighbor's mother was a woman of great faith. One day after being married and having a dozen children, her husband up and left. She waited and prayed for seven years that her husband would come home, and at the end of the seven years, God brought him back. So when asked how long to wait, she would say, "I don't know, but I do know to wait seven years." She had seen the faithfulness of God and could endure patiently.

Is James 1:2-3 a command or an encouragement? Or is James teaching them a new way to think? When we think hardships and trials and tests, we don't automatically say, "Sign me up!" Why? Because they are hard! Trials are a process of purification and advancement. They advance us through a transformation from ourselves into the image of Christ. That is why we should rejoice, because if we succeed, we will be more like Christ. So many friends of mine (after coming out of the hard time) say, "It made me stronger and I would go through it again." But this entails being tested by fire, which is hot and it burns. Physically, after a great workout (if you don't do it very often, like me) our body burns, so why would we do it? Because it will make us stronger, create endurance, and get us in healthier shape. We are soldiers of the Most High. These trials are battles and He wants us in shape for the war that rages.

Some of the finest metals on earth are run through several processes which consist of heating and cooling until the metal is fine enough to be molded into a form of the master's choosing. We must be patient through the trials and endure the fire because that is how we are going to be more like Christ, and we want to emulate His character. One day in 2019 I was praying that God would keep my family and friends from trials, and He told me to not pray that they would avoid them but rather to pray they come out victorious through them. If we avoid them we will not be refined and will not advance to being more like Christ. If we go through them and fail we are set back, but are mercifully given another chance to learn from our mistakes. If we are victorious, then we learned the lesson and are a witness to God's faithfulness.

The victories in God become points of remembrance (ebenezers) to give us strength in future trials. When the disciples were jailed and beaten for Christ's sake, they leapt for joy to have been found worthy to suffer.[5] As I was writing this, I was going through a test of trusting God with my heart, my family, and my country. The guy I thought was perfect for me did not see me as worth it; my good friend was walking away, and I could not do anything about it; and my country was in a pandemic that no one understood. Was it easy to give up those things to God? No, but it was necessary. When I cried over God saying no to the relationship, I would remind myself that God saw me mature enough in Him to be tested in the surrendering of my will, my hope, and my dreams. To be like Jesus is to be moldable, to submit oneself to the design of the Lord, and to bend when He touches us. When going through the trial mentioned, I had to humble myself to be moldable. We don't want to be so hard He has to smash us; we want to be moldable so His hands are always on us, and we are pleasing to Him. God resists a hard heart, but finds pleasure in a heart of (tenderness) flesh.[6]

Trials are never pleasant in the moment,[7] but if we submit to the will of God and allow His work to be developed permanently in us, in time we will find "God has made everything beautiful."[8] Trust in the Lord with all your heart and lean not on your own understanding. In all your ways acknowledge

---

5. Acts 5:41

6. 1 Peter 5:5

7. Hebrews 12:11

8. Ecclesiastes 3:11

Him and He will direct your paths.[9] We rejoice because, if we submit, we have been counted worthy to look more like Christ of whom the Father said, "I am well pleased."[10]

APPLICATION:

What is a trial or testing period that you have recently gone through or are going through right now? I want you to think about it and see how God is forming you into the Christian you are supposed to be, His perfect bride. Write down five things you are grateful for with that trial. This will help us keep our eyes on the goal of alignment with God. If you were not as victorious as you hoped, find your point of failure and write down how to do better next time. There you go, that is one thing to be grateful for: seeing how we can overcome. May the Lord give you encouragement to prepare you for future battles.

---

9. Proverbs 3:5-6

10. 2 Peter 1:17

Alignment When There Is No Answer

"If any of you lacks wisdom, let him ask of God,
who gives to all liberally and without reproach,
and it will be given to him."
James 1:5

We had goats when I was little and we used to give them old bread as a treat after we were done milking them. The bread was stored in a part of the barn where they were not supposed to go behind a closed door with a weak latch. One of my favorite goats broke into the room because she wanted bread right then. But to her demise, she did not wait for me to give it when it was best. She ate the bread and the plastic bag holding the bread, which caused her to suffocate. All she had to do was wait till milking time the next morning. We must trust, if we are not given something we want right away, or if something is taken away, God knew (in His all-knowing power) that whatever it was, was not for our best.

Daniel, in the Bible, set his heart to understand and immediately an angel was sent to him.[11] God does respond to our prayers, sometimes like with Daniel though the message is delayed. As the story goes, God dispatched Gabriel immediately when Daniel prayed, but it took Gabriel twenty-one days to get there because he was having to fight evil spiritual forces on his way. Recently, I have begged God for wisdom because I have hit a wall I cannot reconcile, and I believe He will give it. I have been having trouble understanding why He lets my prodigal friend get away with so much and why my prayers to bring her back have not been answered visually. My prayers have seemed ineffective, and I needed to know how He sees prayer and what it is supposed to be like. One of my bosses literally asks for wisdom with everything he does. He was not a handyman, so as we were fixing a light he asked God for wisdom, and I fixed the light. God does not mind us asking for wisdom, in fact, it brings Him pleasure. Isn't it amazing that God is so good; He wants to give us wisdom, and all we have to do is ask? Ask, seek, knock, find.[12] He is willing if we just humble ourselves and come ask. Sometimes I get caught up in the part where God is the overseer who is making sure all things will ultimately work out for good, and I overlook the fact that God is a giver. A wise parent will not always give you what you want, but they will give you what you need. True wisdom is trusting that He is acting in our best interest and being thankful that He knows and does what is best for us. You may be going through a hard time and think, how is this

---

11. Daniel 10:12

12. Matthew 7:7-8

best? Look to the One who made all things, the One who will help you understand if you seek Him.

He is working to fashion us into Christ's image and He will use everything in our lives to shape and mold us. Sometimes correction is more essential to our transformation than rewards. Other times, saying no to something may just be a test to see if we will apply what we learned and still love Him. We can be wise if we trust that He knows what He is doing and submit ourselves to His work. There was a young woman I knew who was a teacher; she and I were talking about a spiritual test she was going through. As we talked, she said, "I know temptations come from the devil, but why do tests come from God? Does He want us to fail?" I called her by name and said, "How do you know if your students have learned a concept that you have taught?" She sighed as a half-smile spread across her face and said, "A test." For a student, their wisdom can be revealed by a test. For a wise teacher who is analyzing what the students know, testing them can make sure they have acquired wisdom about the lesson. A good teacher is one who wants their students to succeed in the real world, so they test them before they get out there. Mom, before I graduated high school, was always correcting me about little things. One day I asked why and told her my younger siblings needed correction more than I did. While this may have been the case, Mom said that she had the least amount of time with me to get me ready for being an adult in the real world. While we are in the test we ask God for wisdom and victory. He will provide it if we stay aligned with Him.

APPLICATION:

When tests arise I challenge you to praise the Lord because, like the disciples, you have been found worthy and mature enough in your Christian walk to be tested. Also, when hard times and disappointments come, trust in God and ask for wisdom. That prayer is always His delight to answer.

Standing on Christ in Disappointments

"He is a double-minded man, unstable in all his ways."
James 1:8

During the pandemic it was easy to be pulled in two directions. The pastor at the church we were attending struggled with pleasing the maskers and non-maskers. One day in prayer, he said he saw himself testing the wind with his index finger and heard God tell him to decide, make a stand, and stop testing the wind. He was so convicted, he confessed to the whole church and made his stand on what our church would do during the duration of the pandemic. This pastor is an example of both what it looks like to be tempted to be double-minded, but also of what we are to do instead of succumbing to that temptation. He is truly a humble pastor. We should emulate this pastor and stand with God when we are tempted to be double-minded.

This verse in James is in regard to someone who doubts God. As our pastor knows, Christ is our anchor, He keeps us from waning and wavering. If we doubt God is able, who can we put our trust in that will not fail us? People fall short at some point, but Christ never falls short. Sometimes people get disappointed in Christ because He did not deliver as they expected. This can be a disheartening thing. When I was four years old all my older sisters received porcelain dolls for Christmas and I received a pink baby doll who had a hat with bear ears, but my little brain thought it looked like a pig. I was disappointed because my expectation was to receive something beautiful like the others had, not a run-of-the-mill doll. In my comparison I had a pig doll and they had beautiful china dolls. When we look at this as adults, we understand people don't usually give four-year-olds, who are accident prone, a porcelain doll. My parents did not deliver to a four-year-old's expectations. You and I both know that did not mean they failed me. I would get my porcelain doll when I was older and would care for her properly. It is not for us to decide how or when God will answer our prayers, nor was it my place to decide what I got for Christmas. We can ask, and He can say no, but that never means He was not able. It means He had a better way of answering our prayer. On a more adult note, think of those times when our Bible study group wanes and we ask God for more people, we invite more, but no one else comes. Those are the times God is teaching us the valuable lesson of being grateful for the few faithful. Or when we are lonely and ask God for a spouse, but because He does not send one we are able to do great things for God. Kids can ask for cookies, but when we say no because they already had five, this does not mean we do not provide for them. In time, as we mature and trust in the Lord, we will often see, if He allows, the goodness of His plan. Abraham could not see the end of the promise

God made him, but he trusted, and it was accounted to him as righteousness.[13] Just because Abraham did not see it does that mean God failed? Certainly not! We need not doubt nor fret when we ask for something, because He will answer according to His will. And His will is good and best because it is holy. Trust in the Lord with all your heart and lean not on your own understanding, in all your ways acknowledge Him and He will direct your paths.[14] The storms will toss us to and fro, but there is no reason to fear or doubt that He won't do what is best. Stand in Christ. This double-mindedness that James is talking about is doubting the goodness of God and His ability to answer.

APPLICATION:

Aligning ourselves with Christ is difficult when we are disappointed that something did not work out the way we thought it would. For this exercise I want you to take those disappointments and realign with Christ. We do this by taking them before the throne of God in prayer and telling God why we were sad (respectfully, of course). Then we tell Him that we believe He is God, He is good, and we trust Him with this disappointment. We believe that He has done (or will do) what is best for us and we leave it in His capable hands. Thankfulness is a key to standing in peace with Christ.

---

13. Genesis 15:6

14. Proverbs 3:6

"I don't want the devil's bread!" Enduring Through Temptations

"Blessed is the man who endures temptation; for when he has been approved, he will receive the crown of life which the Lord has promised to those who love Him."
James 1:12

When God closed the door on that one relationship that I thought I wanted so badly, He used the experience to teach me something. God showed me that I was wanting a temptation and I had to be like Jesus and say, "I don't want the devil's bread." So, every time my heart longed for this guy, I would shout at the top of my lungs, "I don't want the devil's bread!" That does not mean there was anything wrong with the guy, it just meant that he was not from God for me. This helped me see what I was fighting and it gave me the ability to endure and overcome the temptation of wanting something to which God had said no.

The verse in James tells us that the man is blessed who "endures temptation." The first thing we gather from this is that temptation (dirt and mud) will come and it will be a struggle and a challenge. Enduring is making it through that time when we want another cookie. Now, the temptation James speaks of is definitely something more than cookies, but the same principle is applied: saying no and walking away from something God has not given you includes saying no to John's list of the world's loves: lust of the flesh, the lust of the eyes, and the pride of life.[15] Those are of the world and not from the Father. Before God and I walked through James, we studied the temptation in the wilderness when Jesus was tempted to turn stones into bread. There was nothing wrong with making bread because the fast was over, but the issue was that it was the devil's bread, not God's.[16] We have to trust God to get us through temptations, to come out victorious. When temptation comes say, "I don't want the devil's bread!"

Second, we have to make it through the temptations. We must press on to receive the prize.[17] When God brings us out victoriously, that is when we receive the crown. They say one is blessed because he has made it through, held by God, and did not fall. Christ is there walking through the mud and sludge with us, and when we come out He washes us and gives us a crown. Now, this does not mean we go looking for temptation. If we do that to prove ourselves, we can be sure we will falter, and a righteous man who falters before the wicked is like a murky well.[18] Have no doubt temptation will find us all at

---

15. 1 John 2:16

16. Matthew 4:1-11

17. Philippians 3:14

18. Proverbs 25:26

some point so we must be ready. One time in a women's Bible study one of the ladies went around the room and washed our feet as Jesus did. When she got to me, God showed me that as we run this race of Christianity, we will get dirty from the dust and mud, but to come to Him and He will wash our feet. Ephesians tells us to put on the armor of God so we can stand against the wiles of the devil. Once we have put on the whole armor of God we are instructed to stand.[19] When we stand, the fight will come to us; we have no need to search it out. According to my sister, taking a stand is telling the enemy you are ready for battle. She also says you have got to get your stance right because everything else that you do builds from your stance. In martial arts, we had to learn how to stand and always return to that stance. That was because we needed balance so when the attack came against us, we would not fall as easily. So how do we endure? Stand our ground and fix our eyes on Jesus. We need to only accept our marching orders from Christ, or those whom we know are faithful and trusted messengers; throughout the battle, capture every thought and bring it into submission to the will of God;[20] stand and continue to gather your strength from God, like Jesus did in the wilderness. He stood His ground and reminded Himself what God and His Word said. Be thankful that we are counted worthy to be tested on endurance, don't give up, and pray for victory.

---

19. Ephesians 6:13

20. 2 Corinthians 10:5

APPLICATION:

Even when aligned with God, temptations will come. Don't be caught off guard; trials are normal. Choose now that you will trust God in those times. Trust Him to lead and speak through spiritual leaders in your life. Make a list of people whom you would consider Christian role models. Pray over the names and then ask three to be your spiritual accountability partners. This means sharing your struggles with them and accepting their counsel. Three is to give you more witnesses because the Bible tells us to let everything be established by two or three witnesses.[21] Establish these relationships now, so when temptation comes you will stay anchored.

---

21. Deuteronomy 19:15

DAY SIX

Dying to Be Aligned

"But each one is tempted when he is drawn
away by his own desires and enticed."
James 1:14

At my office there is a small red bird who struggles with this. He sees the glass door that is the pathway to the life of "indoors" and "air conditioning," (which, because he does not have it, must be good). So, he homes in on the door and hopelessly charges it. The glass stops him every time; I know because I hear the thud almost daily. His heart is so set on coming inside, he fails to realize he could live a happier life and a longer one without as much head injury if he quit pursuing his desires and lived the life God made for him. His desire is so consuming it overrides his concern for his health and the damage his flying into the door does to his little body. Aren't we, as humans, sometimes in the same predicament as that little bird?

We will undergo temptation; it is just part of living in this fallen world. Know that we will not be tempted by God—tested yes, but not tempted.[22] The verse above shows us one way temptations come about. We all have desires, like the little red bird, but the temptation is to put those desires above God, which cannot and must not be done. If we believe God is good, sovereign, and does what is best, then we must put that into practice and give Him our desires so they will not supersede His will. We must live in constant submission to Christ. That means trusting He will do what is best and desiring His will above our own. We must walk humbly with the Lord in His path and not desire the air conditioning over where He has made us to live. His path leads to life, while ours is full of sin nature which leads to death.[23] We will be enticed because our will looks really, really, really good to us, and sometimes we get locked into the predator mindset or the addict mindset of "I must have what I desire!" The devil will play on this and try to lock us in so we cannot see anything else, especially God. To walk in God's path we must have a large element of surrender, like Jesus did. When temptation arises we must tell it, "Shut up in Jesus' name! I want God's will!" Or "I do not want the devil's bread!" I have begun saying that since God showed it to me. Let us desire God and all He wants. God is good, He is all good so why do we want to settle for the temptation that is sub-par? The devil offers instant gratification to desires with ultimate death, but Christ offers eternal life to those who wait. Desire heaven and choose life.

---

22. James 1:13

23. James 1:15

APPLICATION:

When these tests and temptations arise give those desires to God. Remind yourself that if God is not in it, no matter how good it looks, you don't want it. Practice now by praying to hunger and thirst for God's will above your own. His Word says you will be filled.[24]

---

24. Matthew 5:6

Fighting Giants

"Then, when desire has conceived, it gives birth to sin; and sin,
when it is full-grown, brings forth death."
James 1:15

Mountain laurel grows by our creek at home, and it is beautiful, but deadly poisonous for consumption. We could race the flowers as little pink and white boats down the water, but when our goats got out and ate some, we had more goats die than at any other time. We knew it was dangerous, but they did not. We treated it as quickly as possible, but their survival depended on how much they ate and how long ago they had eaten it. A little poison will not kill you, but the longer you stay and the more you eat the closer you are to death, physically and spiritually. Typically, our goats knew what was poisonous and what they could eat, but Mountain laurel always, always tricked them. Too often we are like the goats and don't think that this sweet flower could hurt us, but if we do not remain within the parameters God gives us, we will find ourselves consumed by what we consume.

Everyone has desires and the devil pulls on us, enticing us to love and want the desires more than God. There is nothing wrong with desires, but when they compete with Christ, that is when there is a problem. We must be careful to keep our desires in line with the will of God. When they consume us and are our main driving force (like the little red bird from yesterday), we must say "goodbye" to them and again submit ourselves and our hopes to the Lord. Sin begins small and seemingly harmless, but if we don't stop it we will die. When our desires question the goodness of God and are demanding ("I want…") then we must humble our hearts and minds and say, "God's will be done, not mine. Go away in Jesus' name." Yes, it is difficult and hard, but better difficult now instead of eternal death later. I know, while writing this I was certainly tested on this same issue. There was an old desire of meeting someone and getting married that I thought God was going to fulfill for me. I did not go in search of it, but it found me. My problem was I jumped without knowing if it was from God or just a temptation or a test. Some seemingly amazing guy showed up at an event, got my number, and we went out for coffee. On the surface he looked like what I wanted, but it took six months after God closed the door for me to realize he would have destroyed me. The relationship was over long before that, but I still wanted it till God showed me what would have happened had I pursued my will. The good news is our sin can be stillborn. It can be stopped before it kills us like with the goats that we saved. Mine was. I know the struggle, but we cannot give up God's will for ours. King David in his lifetime fought six or seven giants. With age each one became harder for him to beat until one almost killed him.[25] David also had to fight spiritual giants when he stayed home from battle, and he fell when he sinned with Bathsheba.[26] Fight the spiritual giants now while you are still able before they become stronger and you become weaker. Stop the process of submitting to and serving sin by staying under God's authority and submitting yourself to His will, not your own. Remember, this is a trust test. Will we do a "trust fall" with God?

APPLICATION:

What are the giants in your life? What are the temptations you keep struggling with? You need to recognize them now and come up with a game plan on how to overcome. What are the downfalls and how can you use them as opportunities to draw nearer to God and come into alignment with Christ?

---

25. 2 Samuel 21:15

26. 2 Samuel 11

God's Plans Are Best

"Every good gift and every perfect gift is from above,
and comes down from the Father of lights, with whom
there is no variation or shadow of turning."
James 1:17

My sister is a great baker and she planned to make cookies. While she was making the dough, right before the chocolate chips got mixed in, I stole some dough and ate it. Instead of the amazing goodness I was expecting, my mouth was filled with a bitter terrible taste. She had accidentally swapped the sugar for salt. When God gives us something it is right and has "the sugar" in it. But when we fulfill our own desires, when God is not in it, salt has been substituted for sugar and we are left with a bitter taste in our mouths.

Verse fifteen of James chapter one discussed how we can be drawn away by our own desires which lead to sin. Then we are told in verse sixteen to not be deceived because, as verse seventeen explains to us, everything that is good comes from God. James is warning us that just because our desires and plans look good, it does not mean they are. We must trust that God's plans are best. If it is not from God then there is an underlying trap waiting to catch us for evil intent (like the salt). We must not be deceived that what we want is best even though it looks perfect. What Christ does for us has no strings attached; He gives it as a blessing and a gift.

James is also reminding us to acknowledge where good gifts come from and to give thanks for them. We must always love the Giver more than the gift and show our gratitude. In all seasons give thanks for His faithfulness. Teach yourself to know what is of God and what is not. Strive for the things of God and allow the desires that are not His to be nailed to the cross. The cross is where we place everything so we can be like Christ. Paul says, "I am crucified with Christ. Not I who live, but Christ who lives within me."[27] We must wait on God's timing and rest our hope in Him and not the desire. Do not be deceived; what is good, He will give us. What is not good He will keep from us if we are walking in His path. Trust in God.

APPLICATION:

Pray for the discernment to know when we are faced with a gift from God and when we are faced with a temptation from the devil. When we are given a gift, be thankful and enjoy the gift. When it is a temptation, humble yourself and give that desire to God. Nail that bad boy to the cross. And leave it there. You don't want it if it is not from God. Pray that we hunger and thirst for God's will.

---

27. Galatians 2:20

DAY NINE

Love God, Love People

"So then, my beloved brethren, let every man be swift to hear, slow to speak, and slow to wrath."
James 1:19

Have you ever found yourself mentally checking out while someone was talking? I have many times. One time it was on a coffee date. When my sister and I first debated in high school, everyone often used so many facts that we just wanted to check out, but we could not because we needed to understand their case, what angle they were coming from, in order to debate and win. Besides, it would have been rude to check out. In life we need to love people as Christ loves them and listen to them. I find as I get older this is harder, because I see where they are coming from, but I am so focused on the point that I want to drive home, I stop listening and then lose the thread of what they are saying. I'm thinking of what I want to say rather than listening to what they are saying. But we ought not think of ourselves as so important that we must be heard; that is not practicing the mind of Christ.

Listening and being slow to anger are excellent practices for anytime and it takes great humility to not make ourselves be heard and to use self-control to not be enraged by what others say. It is through honor and our love for others that we listen to them. Jesus listened to His elders and was rarely angry. We too ought to listen and give pause before we allow anger to rise inside of us. This is easier said than done. How many of us got angry or were more irritable in 2020 than we used to be? I found myself frustrated with the world, but God called me to love and take the time to listen to others. We had to work harder to keep the mind of Christ. Being slow to speak and slow to anger seems to be encouraging us to exercise patience, self-control, and humility. These are attributes of Christ and our goal should be to look like and live like He did. Philippians gives us an excellent picture of Christ's humility for He humbled Himself twice. Once to come here as a human and the second time He humbled Himself as a human to obey God even when it came to dying.[28] We should practice humility and we can begin by listening and being slow to anger. I bet we will learn something when we listen to people and more importantly, when we listen to God.

APPLICATION:

Begin to practice not interrupting. You want to listen, not cut off. You need to value people enough to hear them out. If we give them that kindness, maybe they will give it to us also. If not, don't get angry, but give them preference. This is not a fun one to practice, but it is a necessary one.

---

28. Philippians 2:5-8

DAY TEN

Watch Your Mouth

"Therefore, lay aside all filthiness and overflow of wickedness,
and receive with meekness the implanted word,
which is able to save your souls."
James 1:21

You may know the old fairy tale in which the servant girl falls into a well where what is in the heart is revealed by what comes out of the mouth. What comes out of the servant girl's mouth is gold and jewels. On the other hand the evil stepsister goes into the well after she sees what happened with her sister, but out of her mouth comes frogs, lizards, and snakes. These were reflections of their hearts. Similarly, our words reflect our hearts.

My sister, when teaching a Bible study, wanted to illustrate this for the girls. She took a bottle of clear water and said, "This is us, but when we allow wickedness to come in, our water is changed." As she spoke these words, she poured instant tea concentrate into the bottle. The water turned from perfectly clear to a murky brown (which if you wanted tea, you would have been happy with, but this was a reflection of what our hearts would do). When our hearts have mixed with filth, it takes gallons of water to clear us up so we will be perfectly clear again. Sometimes it must be dumped out and refilled to make our souls clean again. We must not allow Satan to set up a foothold in our hearts and pollute us.[29]

Scripture tells us a spring cannot have good water and bad come out at the same time.[30] How can we serve God if filth is flying out of our mouths? What is in the heart naturally comes out the mouth.[31] When we find nastiness coming out like spiders, toads, and snakes we need to examine our own heart and be quiet until God changes our heart. When our hearts are not full of Christ, but grime instead, we find the filth pollutes the pure. To avoid this we ought to constantly watch ourselves and come before God asking Him to clean us, like David did in Psalm 51.[32] We must allow God to fill us with the pure water of Christ to wash the sin out of our lives. We can help by hun-gering and thirsting for righteousness because when we do, we will be filled,[33] and if we are filled with righteousness, we will not have room for the filth and wickedness. Then we can pour God's pure water out and be used by God for His glory. Just make sure to go back to God and get refilled.

---

29. Ephesians 4:27

30. James 3:11

31. Matthew 15:18

32. Psalm 51:10

33. Matthew 5:6

APPLICATION:

You are promised as you hunger and thirst for Christ you will be filled. How do you make yourself hungry? You think about the food, you smell the food, you taste the food. So, you should think about the Bread of Life, Christ. Smell Him (read His Word). Taste and see He is good. As you thirst and drink the pure water of Christ you will find Him washing the filth out of your life. Try to catch your behaviors and language before they occur, so to stay clean for God's use.

Aligned with Christ in Service

*"But be doers of the word, and not hearers only,
deceiving yourselves."*
James 1:22

When my siblings and I were little, we lived down a long rocky road. We would ride our bikes up and down, but when we could hear the rocks crackling underneath car tires, the oldest would shout, "Off the road!" You see, when cars were on the road, obedience was required to avoid great injury. Also, in the summer we would play in a creek. The rule was if Mom whistled we all came up on the big rock in the center of the creek. Typically, this was because there was a snake in the water. When Mom whistled it was not the time to find the snake, it was time to obey. A life-and-death moment is not a time to figure out if we want to obey, we need to be in the habit of obedience.

If we are only hearers, how then can we bring glory to God? If we are not in the habit of obeying, then what makes us think we will obey when it really matters? Being only a hearer would be like the parable Jesus told: A man asked both of his sons to go work in his fields; the first said no and the second said yes. However, the second who said yes never did go do it and the first who said no felt so bad that he repented and went to work in the fields.[34] Just because we hear the word of God does not make us followers of Christ. The big question is whether we obey or not. Now we should not tell God no, but instead be hearers and doers. The second son heard the instructions of his father and agreed, but he never obeyed. Jesus said, "If you love Me you will obey Me."[35] Do we love Him or do we just want to hear Him so we can decide if we want to obey or not? Who are we to decide if the words of the King of Kings are to be obeyed? That is so like a child who is weighing the punishment versus the task, but the thing is, we don't see the full punishment. Remember, we are drawn away by our desires. When desire is conceived it gives birth to sin, and sin when it is full grown brings forth death.[36] What kind of servants would we be if we only obeyed when it was convenient? Or better still, what kind of children would we be if we only obeyed when we felt like it? To obey is better than sacrifices.[37] The son who went out and worked anyway, while he might have had the wrong verbal response, he still obeyed. That story gives me hope because so often I don't want to do what God has said, but when I humble myself, I try to submit and obey. However, I ought to obey with a good attitude the first time

---

34. Matthew 21:28-31

35. John 14:15

36. James 1:15

37. 1 Samuel 15:22

and say, "Yes SIR." Trust that what God is asking you to do is best and be doers of the word and not hearers only. Don't stay in the water, get to the Rock.

APPLICATION:

Practice obeying Christ, even in the small things. They may seem silly, but when you obey in the small things you will be trusted with bigger things. What are three areas of your life in which you can begin practicing obedience to Christ?

DAY TWELVE

Alignment Is the Key to Liberty

"But he who looks into the perfect law of liberty and continues in it, and is not a forgetful hearer but a doer of the work, this one will be blessed in what he does."
James 1:25

There was an old sailors' saying that goes, "He who is slave to the compass has the freedom of the seas."[38] Too often we focus on being a slave to the compass without realizing it is because of that knowledge and devotion that we have the freedom of the seas.

Our parents try to teach us the dos and don'ts of society so we will have the keys to success. In the same way, God's law gives us the keys of liberty. Paul often referred to himself as a bondservant of Christ, a forever slave. By being submitted to (bound to) Christ, we have great freedom and liberty both now and eternally. He came to liberate us from sin and death,

---

38. Old sailor's proverb

not subject us to a list of rules. We are able to live without fear and to move in His power (not ours), which gives us liberty to go places and do things we never would have imagined. Writing, for example, was something no one would have ever imagined me doing. I was the one who hated reading, would not sit still for any amount of time beyond what was necessary, and was a doer, not a writer. I wanted my handwriting to be like my big brother's (which it is, be careful what you wish for); my sisters have cute or beautiful handwriting and mine is boyish. I also did not enjoy grammar. Most of my other siblings acquired skills in writing, but God decided to have me be the first one to publish a Bible study. His path for us is way beyond our imagination.

The perfect law of liberty. The first time I really read this I thought it was an ironic statement to have a law of liberty. The law sounds like a set of binding rules where liberty sounds like freedom and no restraints. However, liberty is more than just freedom. It is having the law, knowing the boundaries of the law, and having the freedom to do good. Proverbs says whoever fears the commandment will have life.[39]

God will guide us to use the liberty He gives to accomplish His will. Christ's examples show us the great good we are free to do. Even God giving us the law is to liberate us. When we know the rules we can know how to live within them. Rule one: Love God with all your heart, soul, mind, and strength. Rule two: Love your neighbor as yourself. These two sum up all the laws and the prophets.[40]

---

39. Proverbs 13:13

40. Matthew 22:37-40

APPLICATION:

May the Lord give you the humility to become a slave to the compass. Lord, tether our hearts to Your law. Give us the understanding of liberty in You. Please give us the will to fight to align our souls with Yours. Now pray to willingly walk in the Law of Liberty.

Our Words Affect Our Witness

"If anyone among you thinks he is religious,
and does not bridle his tongue but deceives his own heart,
this one's religion is useless."
James 1:26

Our tongue seems to be one of the hardest muscles to gain control over. I know because I have been a talker my whole life. My siblings and I have a joke that I came out talking. While talking can be a great encouragement to others, if we do it too much sometimes it is hard to stop the words from coming out when we are on a roll. Once I heard it explained like toothpaste. We can easily squeeze it out, but putting it back is virtually impossible. When I was young, I actually told someone they were not photogenic because I did not know what it meant. I thought it was fearing the camera. Many times, I have wished I could take back those words because I did not mean them, and they were said to one of the sweetest ladies I know. But they cannot be taken back and it is almost, almost impossible to stop the damage of words. Words cannot go back into your mouth.

As we walk this path toward Jesus, each step we take brings us closer and we become more and more transformed into His image; bridling our tongue is part of that. Jesus only did and said what He saw and heard the Father doing.[41]

If we don't slip up in word, then we are able to control any part of ourselves.[42] This is a great place to start learning self-control. Everything that we say and do ought to be brought under the submission of Christ. Unless we allow ourselves to be formed by Christ, we will not be any farther along in our faith than we were when we got saved, which means our faith would be sedentary. If we are sedentary then we become stagnant. Out in the country if you leave a bucket out it will fill with rain. If it is not dumped out the water will become stagnant and mosquitoes will grow in it. They inevitably hatch, attack your arms and legs, and you itch till it hurts. Same way with our Christianity. If we leave it alone and don't do something with it, it only creates a place for either complacency or hypocrisy to grow, either of which in turn causes pain to those around us. Paul says he presses on toward the prize of glory set before him, choosing to not be sedentary, but constantly moving.[43] We can't hold still in our faith. We must allow the Holy Spirit to stir us and convict us so that we may grow. Stagnant water does not taste good to anyone and only hateful mosquitoes and nasty bacteria grow there.

---

41. John 5:19

42. James 3:2

43. Philippians 3:13-14

However, flowing water, running water, fresh water delights the soul of thirsty and weary travelers. As we move and grow with God, we will delight the souls of others and most importantly we delight His soul, so let's grow closer to Christ and start bridling our tongues.

APPLICATION:

James seems to talk a lot about the tongue. Try to curb running your mouth. It is a huge battleground because what God's people say can smear His character. Instead of reviling (speaking rudely), determine in your heart to either speak life or not speak at all.

Next Level of Being Unspotted

"Pure and undefiled religion before God and the Father is this: to visit orphans and widows in their trouble, and to keep oneself unspotted from the world."
James 1:27

W e all should care for orphans and widows but, we cannot do everything, and sometimes God calls us to wait because He is asking someone else to obey. To illustrate this I am going to share with you one of my biggest failures. We were at church and there was an altar call. The pastor's wife went to pray and was weeping over something. I could watch the pastor rocking back and forth. He would begin to head his wife's direction and then pull back. I know why. He yearned to help and pray for her, but God was telling him "No," and he was obeying. This was a test for me that I failed. God would say, "Go, pray for her," and I would say, "No." After going over this several times, from the corner of my eye I saw my sister leave the pew and pray over this precious woman. Then I told God, "Okay, now I'll go," and He said, "No. I have given it to another." I cannot describe the sinking feeling that was in my stomach when He said those words to me. Realize the pastor was told to refrain, and I was told to go. The lesson here is to obey whether you are told "No" or "Go." We must use discernment to know whom we can and are supposed to help. Pure religion is caring for others and making sure we are right with God.

Our standards and God's standards are so different; He always takes it to the highest level. When the disciples were taking care of the widows in Acts there was an issue that arose because the Hellenist widows were not being taken care of. Because of this the disciples chose men from among them to specifically handle caring for these women.

Often, I have heard the first half of this verse, but we must not throw out the last part even if it is hard: keeping oneself unspotted from the world. We keep ourselves unspotted by being washed by Jesus and by obeying Him. What James is saying sounds a lot like the two greatest commandments: Love God with all your heart and love your neighbor as yourself.[44] We don't have to do a wondrous work or something huge and courageous to be unspotted; Christ already did that on the cross.[45] What He wants from us is simply love, service, and obedience. If we love Christ we will obey Him;[46] caring for widows and orphans is a part of serving Him. And as we do to the least of these, we have done to Him.[47] Make sure to obey.

---

44. Matthew 22:37-40

45. 1 John 2:2

46. John 14:23

47. Matthew 25:40

APPLICATION:

May you not fail as I did that Sunday. Resolve in your heart to obey God and pray for His grace to do it. You will fall at some point; all have, but remember the righteous man will fall, but he will rise again by God's grace.[48] Be humble to obey the call of God to "go" or "stay," but do it in obedience.

---

48. Proverbs 24:16

Overflowing and Pouring Out Christ

"My brethren, do not hold the faith of our
Lord Jesus Christ, the Lord of glory, with partiality."
James 2:1

When you were little did your mom ever ask you to water the plants? Mom asked my little brother one day and he watered everything, even the sidewalk. He did not care what got wet, because he was just watering. Christ ought to be such a huge part of our lives that He is shared whenever we meet someone. And we should be so joyous we don't care who gets watered by Jesus because we are just watering.

When we are full of Jesus, we should be overflowing with Him. If we are zealously pouring out wherever, then there is no reserve regarding who gets touched by Christ. He did not come to die for just one person or one set of people, nor does He love anyone less. Christ came so that anyone who would believe in Him could have life and life abundantly.[49] It is not our job to decide who goes to heaven or hell. Our job is to love God with all that we are and make disciples of all men.[50, 51] Whether or not they choose to live for Christ is on them, but did we represent Christ to them well? Did they get wet by being around us?

When I was little, Mom taught me that everyone was watching and so I needed to behave myself in a manner that pleased God, honored Him, and honored my father. When Christ tells us to move we must obey. Like when we discussed the pastor being told to wait and me being told to move. Be like the pastor who obeyed. Don't tell the Holy Spirit why something is not a good idea. If we did that we would be disobedient and prideful servants because we think we know better than our Lord. We ought to walk in humility as Christ did. Be full of faith and the Holy Spirit, so that anyone who comes near you gets a part of Jesus' overflow from you. We need to be like Stephen in the Bible. He was one of those chosen to feed the widows in the book of Acts.[52] You might be called "holier than thou," because Christ is always on your heart, mind, and mouth, but as long as you are right with God, don't worry about it and let the overflow continue. "He who believes in Me, as the Scripture has said, out of his heart will flow rivers of living water."[53]

49. John 10:10

50. Matthew 22:37

51. Matthew 28:19

52. Acts 6:1-6

53. John 7:38

APPLICATION:

Does Christ come up in your everyday conversations? My grandmother was, sadly, not living like a Christian. Instead of pounding her over the head with the Bible, I chose to write her letters about what God was doing in my life. My goal was to graciously give her as much of Jesus as possible. I made a point when I told her about accomplishments to accredit them to God's grace. But as I wrote those letters I thought, shouldn't He come up like that in all my conversations, not just when I am trying to witness to someone? So, I challenge you to make and talk about Christ everywhere in your life. He is our savior, our hero, so why is He not in all our conversations? It might sound weird at first, but keep at it and it will become a habit.

DAY SIXTEEN

Heart of the Father

"If you really fulfill the royal law according to the Scripture,
'You shall love your neighbor as yourself,' you do well."
James 2:8

Over this past year I have experienced many relational hardships. Some were betrayals when my friends left me for someone who did more exciting things. Some were old friends who just quit talking to me. A Bible study I facilitated broke up, and a very close friend left to chase the things of this world. As I was getting angry for the offenses against me, I learned my response was not like Christ's. Through that I learned I did not know how to love. I found myself being the older brother of the prodigal son. I did not have the heart of the Father. That is what loving our neighbor is about, having the heart of our Father.

Do we really love our neighbor as ourselves? I still don't love as I should. Jesus said to love God with all that we are and to love our neighbors. On those two principles hang all the laws and the prophets.[54] If we would practice these two concepts, I believe we would be able to walk rightly before the Lord and not shame His name by being unloving. James is instructing the reader to not show partiality but to love all people in order to bless God's name. Even if they berate us, we still must act like Christ. If we practice this, few people should be able to bring reproach to God about our behavior.

Now love is not the acceptance of bad and sinful behavior. It is not showing partiality to people and it is correcting them in love when you see them stumbling. The Lord corrects those He loves.[55] We ought not to be afraid to encourage one another in the Lord and to help them keep the path of life. Furthermore, we ought to ask God to show us how He sees people. Remember, have the heart of the Father. We do not judge by outward appearance, but look at the heart as God does. Even Samuel the prophet was looking at the outside when God sent him to choose King David. God told him to stop looking at appearance because God looks at the heart.[56] We want our hearts to be pure and clean before Him. We want them to be a mirror of His own heart. If we find that our hearts are not right before God, then we ought to pray as David did: "Create in me a clean heart, O God, and renew a steadfast spirit within me."[57] This is why David was a man after God's own heart—when he was out of alignment with God, he humbled himself to get his heart right again.

---

54. Matthew 22:40

55. Hebrews 12:6-11

56. 1 Samuel 16:7

57. Psalm 51:10

APPLICATION:

Ask yourself, "Do I have the heart of the Father?" Ask Him, and He will gently guide you in the path you should go. Follow Him where He leads. Write down what He shows you when you ask.

Living in Liberty and Being Faithful

"So speak and so do as those who will be judged by the law of liberty."
James 2:12

I have observed many people who have been liberated from some addictions, but they fall back into bondage and sin when they find themselves back in similar circumstances. My sister knew one girl who had been freed several times from an abusive and immoral life, but even though God had set her free, she kept returning. She had to realize that we must be vigilant and flee temptation. She had to learn that in order to keep herself free, she needed to maintain a rigorous unyielding schedule to avoid being in the same environment. She eventually realized that she needed to exercise a lot of self-discipline to avoid the temptation.

Since we have been freed from sin and from the condemnation of the law, we ought to live like it and not go back to the ways of the flesh. Because Christ died for us we now have power to walk in the Spirit and not fulfill the lusts of the flesh.[58] With Christ in us we are given strength and the freedom to not revert to the ways of the old man.[59] We are given access to the fruits of the Spirit and freedom to use self-control. Have we lived for Christ and lived as new creations walking in the spirit and not in the flesh? Or have we gone back to the chains because they were comfortable and familiar? Did we put back on the old dead man and disregard the sacrifice that set us free? All have sinned and fallen short of the glory of God,[60] but now we are liberated from the law of sin and death,[61] so what have we done with our liberty?

Jesus once told a parable about three men who were each given a bag of money, talents, according to what the master knew was their ability to use the wealth wisely.[62] They each had the liberty to do with the money as they saw fit, but they would have to give an account for their actions. They would be punished for doing something wrong with it and rewarded for doing well with it. This was fair and reasonable. The money was a loan to them. Their master was testing them with his treasure. Two doubled their money and gave it back to their master. One hid it and only gave the master back what was his. Like the servant with the talents, what have we done with the gift we have been entrusted with? Have we used it to further God's Kingdom or did we bury it? We should use the liberty

---

58. Galatians 5:16

59. Colossians 3:9-11

60. Romans 3:23

61. Romans 8:2

62. Matthew 25:15

of freedom to do what is right, never what is wrong, but we must work hard to pursue our freedom, and we must use our freedom well for God's service. With the fear of God, we can do this. The fear of the Lord is the beginning of wisdom; all who follow His precepts have good understanding.[63]

APPLICATION:

Where have you walked back to chains that used to hold you captive? When He does free you, it is your job to run out of them and run to Him. Never go back to the chains. This is a fight for your soul to be in alignment with Christ. Recognize the areas where you have begun to head back to the chains and flee! Ask God for a plan to flee from temptation and then ask for the strength to implement it.

---

63. Psalm 111:10

Pumping Our Faith Into Action

"Thus also faith by itself, if it does not have works is dead."
James 2:17

The first time I rode my two-wheeler bike there was the thought that this was impossible to pump with my legs, balance on two wheels, move forward, and steer all at the same time. But as I did it over and over again, my confidence grew. In the same way, as we see God prove Himself over and over again, we gain more confidence in His faithfulness.

A body without a beating heart will die. It loses all its color, becomes ashen, and because life no longer flows through it, it can do nothing but rot. This is how our Christianity is when works are not the evidence of our faith. Works pump our faith into action and our faith lives and grows. Without pumping our faith into action, it is simply words and thoughts. If we have faith without action, then nothing has been accomplished for the kingdom as if we just thought about riding the bike without actually doing it.

Yet, when we move on the path we believe God has asked us to travel, our faith is put into action and we are feeding our spiritual bodies; therefore, work to show yourself approved.[64] When we are traveling in faith and He blocks a path, we will likely get discouraged, but remember to be humble and trust that He blocks it for a reason. Keep pumping! Look for the next path He will open. Setbacks happen; tires go flat; paths close; that is when we regroup and come at it again. On his missionary travels Paul tried many paths, until God opened the right one.[65] We will often grow weary, but when that happens come to the Lord and He will give you rest.[66] He will give us a daily dose of strength that will get us through the day. Now, our energy will be spent by the end of the day, but it will be enough to get us through. Just come to the source of life that you may continue to pump out good works. Grow your faith by reflecting on what God has done and then continue to pump faith out and serve Him in faith, knowing that something good for the kingdom is coming out of it. All work is profitable.[67]

APPLICATION:

Faithfulness is something that is not practiced as it should be anymore. Will you be faithful to Christ and obey Him, or will you just talk about it? Is action backing your words or do you just talk about Jesus? When you believe God has called

---

64. 2 Timothy 2:15

65. Acts 16:6-10

66. Matthew 11:28-30

67. Proverbs 14:23

you to something, and it has been confirmed through spiritual authorities, practice putting it into action. If you aren't at that place with God yet, then begin putting into action what God calls you to do in the Bible. You say you believe it, then do it. Pick one principle in the Bible to put into action.

Good Works = Evidence of Alignment

"But someone will say, 'You have faith, and I have works.'
Show me your faith without your works,
and I will show you my faith by my works."
James 2:18

I love the smell of coffee in the morning; it is a childhood memory. Coffee comes from the beans being crushed and having hot, boiling water run through them. When I open a bag or can of coffee, I stick my head in the container so I can get a good relaxing breath of the smell of coffee. People can tell when another person is drinking coffee because the liquid in the cup bears the same smell, color, and taste of the coffee beans. Can others tell when we have been changed by Christ? The water has been permanently changed by the beans. Do we smell like, bear the same image as, and taste like Christ to those who encounter us? Can people tell by what we say and do that we belong to Christ? It is like coffee in the morning.

Works are the evidence of faith (just like coffee is the evidence of the coffee bean). Because we believe God, we do His works. Faith sometimes can be like standing in a mist or a fog and hearing a still small voice. But works is choosing to trust that voice and walk in the fog and not just stand still; the still small voice is calling us to move forward. If we only hear we will never find our way out of the fog. Likewise, if we only hear God's correction and never change our behavior, some will wonder if we are really Christians or not.

Is our mind the mind of Christ, and is it governed by His will?[68] Does He have all of our heart, soul, mind, and strength so we believe and act like Him?[69] We must do all of the above. As Paul says, we are to be crucified with Christ so it is no longer we who live, but Christ who lives in us.[70] This happens when He is our faith, He is our works, and we give Him all of us. Faith is the substance of things hoped for, the evidence of things unseen.[71] Works are the evidence of faith and show the unseen. When we walk in faith and in good works, the unseen God and His ways become visible.

APPLICATION:

Do your words and actions coincide with each other, or do they send conflicting messages? Get a close, honest, Christian friend and the two of you watch each other. If both your words and actions agree and bring glory to God, keep up the good work. If they don't, then you know your application: change.

---

68. Philippians 2:5

69. Mark 12:30

70. Galatians 2:20

71. Hebrews 11:1

What Do Our Actions Say of Our Alignment?

"You believe that there is one God. You do well.
Even the demons believe and tremble!"
James 2:19

When I was in high school we did a ropes course. It was terrifying. Perhaps the most terrifying was the zipline. I climbed up a power pole and walked across another one to get to a tiny platform. From there I was supposed to jump off the unsteady platform and trust a rope to not break with my dead weight dropped on it. I saw it hold boys twice or three times my weight, so I believed it should hold me. But if I had not put my action behind those beliefs and jumped, then I would still be on that terrifying, wabbly platform. Has believing in Christ changed us? Has it caused us to jump off and trust Him to hold us? Has our belief caused us to put action behind our reasoning or just caused us to contemplate some more?

Have we given over our desires and wants to be crucified with Christ, or are we still chasing our iniquities? The demons know who He is and they are afraid, but that does not change anything about them. They still chase their own iniquities. James tells us it is not enough to simply believe. Remember, faith without works is dead. If our actions do not support our faith then where is our witness? It would be like paper money not backed by gold. It becomes worth less and less; eventually it can do nothing, and is only good for the fire. Are we living as followers of Christ? Is our faith backed by action? Do the marks of Christianity follow us? Faith, hope, and love are fruits of the Spirit, but also included are: kindness, longsuffering, things people often can see more easily. These are marks of Christianity.

What are we living for? If our answer is something other than Christ, then we need to change how we are living. When we live for Christ, we act on our beliefs that He is God, that He is good, that He deserves our best in every aspect of our lives: mind, will, and emotions. We believe He deserves to be obeyed and He wants every heart, mind and soul.[72] But belief is just a thought if it is not accompanied with an action. So, how do we have an active life of belief?

Ask God to teach you. He says if we lack wisdom to ask, and He will give it.[73] Be moldable and humble. Don't be afraid of the Christian life. Jump off that platform into the arms of Jesus; He has got you. Many have gone on before us, and they

---

72. Matthew 22:37

73. James 1:5

are examples for us to follow. Faith without works is dead.[74] "All things work together for good to those who love God, to those who are the called according to His purpose."[75] In all things work for the glory and good of God who loves us.

APPLICATION:

Where are we still walking in our iniquities? If we believe He is God we need to give Him our all. Target these areas of iniquity (self-serving) and come up with a battle plan to bring them into alignment with Christ. We don't want to just know He is God, we want to live like we believe it.

---

74. James 2:14-17

75. Romans 8:28

Trust God in His Path

"Was not Abraham our father justified by works
when he offered Isaac his son on the altar?"
James 2:21

When I was eight, my grandmother gave us Christmas money. I bought a doll and a pink Precious Moments Bible. But before I bought it, Mom told me that she was going to buy me one with my name engraved on it, but she left the choice up to me. I did not want to let go of the Bible I found, and therefore I never received the engraved Bible. While this is a childish story, it still portrays the childish thinking that is in all of us when we think that what we have is better than what God wants to give us.

Abraham was justified by works because works are the testimony of our faith. We should trust and obey God when we know what He has asked us to do. Even though sacrificing the promised and long-awaited son did not make sense,

Abraham heard God and obeyed.[76] We too must give God our hopes, dreams, promises, hearts, all of it, all of us. We live to bring glory to Christ. When we hold onto things and don't give them to God, then we are saying we cannot trust what He does is good. Jesus said the greatest commandment is to love God with all your heart, mind, soul, and strength.[77] Are we all in or do we just talk the talk without walking the walk? Will we give Him the generic Bible for the one He has waiting for us? Or trust Him when it looks like we have to give Him the beautiful one and accept a generic one? Will we put actions behind our words and trust Him? I was talking with some girls one day and we discussed God closing doors because He had something better for us and one of the girls said, "You left a door that He was closing because He has a gorgeous door for you." And my sister and I both said, "Maybe not." Not that whatever God brought was not good, but sometimes it is not glamorous. Sometimes it is a plain brown door and He wants to see if we will trust Him by walking through it even though it does not look as fun. When my mom toured Rome in college, she and her sister went to an old cathedral. From the outside, it looked like a plain, humble building, but once inside the building turned into a magnificent masterpiece. God does not always give us the lovely path—just look at the heroes of the faith—but He always asks us to trust Him and see that He is enough.

If we grew up in church, we can fake it to the world because we know the lingo. We know all those Bible verses and

---

76. Genesis 22:1-3

77. Mark 12:30

Christian clichés. God does not want halfhearted Christians. Halfhearted Christians will obey in the time when it benefits us, but when Christ asks for something hard like sacrifice, or a plain brown door, we try and wait God out. Maybe if I wait long enough, He will change His mind. For example, nagging Mom and Dad for something. We ask and wait and ask again and again. How can we think that we can outsmart God and outwait the Eternal One? Sometimes it works with our parents, but we cannot trick God. Balaam was a man whose story is found in the book of Numbers. He wanted to outwait God so he could get what he wanted. He had been offered more money than he could ever need to curse God's people. He begged God and eventually, God let him go. Balaam did not want to give up the money and fame to obey God, so as he went on his way in disobedience, God sent an angel to kill him before he could ever spend the money. On his way to curse God's people, the donkey he was riding saw the angel who was sent to kill Balaam. Three times the donkey evaded the angel, but on the third time Balaam got mad because the donkey was being obstinate. God opened the donkey's mouth to speak and then God opened Balaam's eyes to see what the donkey was trying to save him from. If it was not for the donkey the story would have just been: There was a man named Balaam who begged God to have it his own way and when God said fine, Balaam died on his own path. But instead we have a story where God teaches a man that no amount of money can make it okay to disobey God. Nothing is too great a sacrifice to give to God.

No one likes the pain that can come with good works, but the outcome is always growth which brings us closer to the person God wants us to be. Pain causes us to dig deep and see what we are made of. It causes us to see where our hope and trust rests. If we reinstate and reaffirm Christ as our hope and sanctify Him in our hearts, then we will come out victorious. Jesus prayed in the garden to have the cup pass from Him, but nevertheless God's will be done.[78] Paul prayed for the thorn in the flesh to be removed, but God said, "My grace is sufficient."[79] It is okay to appeal, but when the answer is given we must obey through thick and thin. We cannot be flippant and only decide to obey when it is pleasant. Christ suffered in obedience. We should expect no different. When David pleaded for the life of his child and God took that life and gave His answer, David worshiped.[80] That is what we are to do when God gives His answer. God does not want us to be fair weather, halfhearted Christians. We must let our salvation and hope be built on the Rock so we will not waver with the storms, but learn that without the storms we will not know what God can get us through. Lord, give us the strength to obey and when we can't run, please run for us. When our minds lose their focus please restore them by bringing us back to You.

APPLICATION:

Pray for God to help you accept, obey, and endure. When you find yourself trying to outwait God, even though His will has been confirmed through witnesses, STOP. Humble yourself and realign with His will.

---

78. Luke 22:42

79. 2 Corinthians 12:7-10

80. 2 Samuel 12:20

Freedom in Alignment

I feel the need to go over James 2:12 again from another point of view.

*"So speak and so do as those who will be
judged by the law of liberty."*

Before I was born, my sister who was about two-years-old was given freedom to walk on the stairs of a pool while the older ones played, but only on the stairs because she could not swim yet. The rules were there to protect her. But she was not free to go beyond the stairs. However, she, as a human, even at such a young age has the freedom and ability to make decisions. So she pushed the limits and was caught in a current and swept into the shallow end of the pool. Mom or Dad had her out of the water in a very short amount of time, but she had already ingested so much water, she had become unconscious. My sister says she had drowned. Praise the Lord for the lady who was there because she revived and woke my sister back up (I assume through CPR, but again I was not born yet).

The rules were there to protect my sister from that happening, but she had the freedom to do what was right and stay or to disobey and risk death.

I have recently heard liberty defined as the freedom to do what is right. This definition is profound. Too often we define and think of liberty as the freedom to do whatever we want, or as liberty being without the restraint of the law. However, the most beautiful definition I have ever heard is the one of liberty being the freedom to do what is right. We never have the freedom to do what is wrong or think we are above the law. Not having the right definition of the law of liberty was my problem when trying to reconcile the idea in my brain because I was trying to reconcile having freedom to do as I pleased with living the Christian life in submission to God. Before Christ came we were caught in the cords of our sin[81] and could do nothing right. But God sent His only begotten Son to die for us that whoever believes in Him would not perish but have everlasting life.[82] When Christ died He set us free from being hell bound and also made it possible for us to choose right. He gave us the freedom to do what is right. Because we have been given this liberty we are responsible to use it. Practice and get into the habit of doing good. If it is in our power to do good and we do not do it, it is considered a curse to us.[83] The law of liberty is the freedom to do what is right. So how will we answer if given the opportunity and we do not take it? Jesus

81. Proverbs 5:22

82. John 3:16

83. James 4:17

Himself said, "Just as you want men to do to you, you also do to them likewise."[84]

APPLICATION:

Now that you know you have the freedom to do what is right, what is it that God is calling you to do in this freedom? Freedom took a price, doing what is right will also take a price, but we pay that price gladly in alignment with God.

---

84. Luke 6:31

Bitter or Lemonade

"Do you see that faith was working together with his (Abraham's) works, and by works faith was made perfect?"
James 2:22

There was a girl I ministered to at a pregnancy center. At the time, she was turned off to Christ because of the hypocrisy of His people. Most of our time together was spent not on preparing her for the baby in her, but tending to the starving baby in her spirit that was dying. God had to reaffirm His truth, and I apologized to this young woman on behalf of the hypocrites because we are not all like that. We must work hard not to be hypocrites. Do our words and actions portray to the world who we say Christ is?

Works complete faith. Obedience is the evidence of our beliefs. A test offers evidence that the students have learned the lesson. Up to the test the teacher has faith that the students are learning, but the test is proof. Jesus said you are the light of the world so let your light shine before men that they may see your good works and glorify your Father in heaven.[85] Others should see Christ in us by what we say and do; both are necessary for a glorifying witness. Because He is living in us, He should be bubbling out of us, fulfilling good works through our hands and feet. However, in order to work through us we must be a willing vessel. If we are not a willing participant in God's work, we could deaden the intended effects or quench the Spirit. No one likes to work with someone who does not want to be there. Neither does God. He chooses to pour Himself into those who are willing, so we should choose to be willing so our faith will be made perfect. If we don't act on our beliefs and faith then they are dead and nothing more than thin air. When that happens people assume we are hypocrites. People want to believe what we say about Christ is real, but too often they don't because we fail to put into practice what we preach. Paul says woe to teachers because they will be held responsible to live up to the standard they teach.[86] If they don't line up, we are giving conflicting messages and our witness is still-born, or worse, aborted. We want a perfect witness and healthy baby. By two or three witnesses let things be established.[87] Our words and actions are two witnesses. What do they say? When we don't put into practice what we say, then it is like the righteous who falter before the wicked, like a murky and polluted well. Which do you want to be and which are you?

---

85. Matthew 5:16

86. James 3:1

87. Deuteronomy 19:15

APPLICATION:

Will you be like Abraham? If you have not noticed, alignment and obedience are coinciding a lot. Where are you giving conflicting messages? How are you doing on overcoming it? How can you do better? Make a list and begin aligning your words and actions with Christ.

Friend's Status with God

*"And the Scripture was fulfilled which says, 'Abraham believed
God, and it was accounted to him for righteousness.'"*
James 2:23

When we were walking through a painful situation with my good friend being a prodigal, we were in a Bible study where God had sent us a future missionary. Some nights it was just two of my sisters, the future missionary, and myself. By walking that year together, we became very close friends because we poured out our hearts to each other regarding this mutual friend and built each other up in the Word. She poured into us, and we poured into her and over time we all earned the status of very, very good friends.

There are three men in the Old Testament who had a relationship with God that we might want to emulate: Abraham (friend of God),[88] Moses (whom God spoke to face to face),[89]

---

88. James 2:23

89. Exodus 33:11

and David (a man after God's own heart).[90] Wow, to be called righteous and the friend of God.[91] Jesus said to His disciples, I no longer call you disciples, but friends.[92] How do we get there? How do we move to friend status instead of acquaintance? It happens after we have proven ourselves to be trustworthy, to be on a closer level with God. When we were little we had to practice obeying even without knowing why. Once we got older our parents explained more to us. As we have grown, we have been given more leeway to offer suggestions to our parents, because we have been found trustworthy enough. Mom is still Mom, and I respect and obey her, but now we are close friends who discuss decisions and concerns. Likewise, Amos says, God does nothing without telling His servants the prophets.[93] When Abraham believed and obeyed, he proved himself trustworthy. In a friendship both parties do what is best for the other. God has always got our best in mind. He sent His Son to die so we might live.[94] His ways and thoughts are higher than the heavens above the earth compared to ours.[95] So how do we do what is best for God? We obey Him. We have just discussed how faith without works is dead,[96] and how when we say one thing and do another it

---

90. 1 Samuel 13:14

91.James 2:23

92. John 15:15

93. Amos 3:7

94. 1 John 4:9

95. Isaiah 55:8-9

96. James 2:17

is like a polluted well.[97] This brings shame and a bad name to ourselves and to God. To do what is best for God is to seek to please Him, to put His will above ours and obey Him because we believe Him to love us, to be good and to do what is best for us. Doing what is best for God will result in our best. As we come to this mindset and prove our trustworthiness by obedience, we too can be called friends of God. "As for God, His way is perfect; the word of the Lord is proven. He is a shield to all who trust in Him."[98]

APPLICATION:

As you go about your day and you come to a decision point, pause and ask yourself, "What is best for God?" Don't worry about what is best for you because God is always watching out for you.

---

97. Proverbs 25:26

98. 2 Samuel 22:31

Practice What You Preach

"My brethren, let not many of you become teachers,
knowing that we shall receive a stricter judgment."
James 3:1

Teachers receive a stricter judgment because they have taught others in the way of life; therefore, they have no excuse when they do not practice what they teach. When we teach others we will be tested. We were putting on a singles' conference and the part I taught was about trusting in God and giving up what we want. Sure enough the test was waiting in the audience. I wanted to get married and I began to play with the idea more than keeping my eyes on God. There was a young man whom we will call "Temptation," and I spent the next six months in heartache trying to trust God, accept what His plan was, and give up my childhood dream as He closed the door to that Temptation. The guy at the time seemed perfect for me, but God knew better. It was still hard to let God take him out of my hands, but God, in His time opened my eyes to see truth. God knows that we are only human, but to whom much is given, much is expected.[99] Teachers have been given wisdom and knowledge, so when trials come we are expected to apply what we have taught and been taught. If we don't live it, then our witness is shot and we go back to faith without works being dead. If we don't apply the teachings God has given us we are like the righteous who falter before the wicked.[100] We call them hypocrites today, a dead witness. Can God use dead, dry bones to teach?[101] Yes, but He can do more with living ones. Jesus told the disciples to do what the Pharisees taught, not what they did.[102] We don't want that to be said about us. Teachers should know better. Because of this, teachers must be humble and moldable by God and those He sends (even if it be a child). We never want to go beyond the mindset of learning from God. Sometimes I must remind myself that God still uses donkeys like in the story of Balaam from Day Twenty-Two, and we must apply ourselves to listen instead of pushing for our own way like Balaam did. All Christians must be seeking to grow closer to God, and when seeking we must also be willing to change to His image and His will, to exemplify His name. We are not to be conformed to this world, but be transformed by the renewing of our minds that by testing we may discern what is the will of God.[103] This life is about our spirits being transformed to the image of Christ; even more so as teachers of truth.

---

99. Luke 12:48

100. Proverbs 25:26

101. Ezekiel 37:1-14

102. Matthew 23:3

103. Romans 12:2

APPLICATION:

We have been given the keys to victory in Christ: humility, love, and obedience. How can you apply these into your life, to walk in victory? Begin by praying for these things and ask the Holy Spirit to quicken your heart to see when you fail so you can recover.

Aligning the Tongue

"Even so the tongue is a little member and boasts great things.
See how great a forest a little fire kindles!"
James 3:5

Many years ago my sister and I were driving home and I was talking, pouring out my heart, being vulnerable. She said something short and sharp that hurt me to the core of my heart. She apologized within fifteen minutes, and I know it was fifteen minutes because I can tell you where we were and what we were passing when the pain was inflicted and where we were when it was apologized for and forgiven. Forgiveness chases away bitterness, but pain can be different.

I can hear my mom saying, "Watch what you say," or the words from that old song, "Be careful, little mouth, what you say." We are given mouths to exhort, lovingly correct fellow believers, speak truth, and praise God. But so easily this little mouth becomes a big mouth, and what God intended to be a tool for life becomes an instrument of destruction or death. You know that old saying, "Sticks and stones can break my bones, but words can't hurt me"? This saying is wrong. For me, words last much longer than a bruise. They go down into the heart of its victim and take up residence if that person does not know how to give their pain to God. When given the chance, speak life, not death. Our time here on this earth is so short; be careful what you say and think about it before you say it. Peter and Paul both tell us to use this time here on earth to redeem the time we lost while serving ourselves before we began to seek God. Once words are spoken they cannot be retracted. Thankfully the damage may be repaired like with my sister, but the words cannot be unsaid. Sometimes pain from a wound, even a verbal one, can last a long time. I suppose that is so God can keep it fresh so we will remember the lesson longer. Also, pain can make us more cautious and careful with others.

We see how our words and actions affect others, as well as our witness. Remember what we say will be tied back to Christ. We want Him to have the good name that He deserves and we want to represent His character truthfully to the world. Remember the basics: What would Jesus do? Whether in word or deed, let us do all to the glory of God.[104] Think of the lasting consequences of your actions and words before they come out of you. The little things matter. We will all mess up at some point, but know that he who controls his own tongue can control the rest of his body,[105] just like an entire ship is controlled by a small little rudder that dictates the way the ship will sail. So, think and pray first for the right words.

---

104. Colossians 3:17

105. James 3:2

APPLICATION:

Practice avoiding negative words. Correction is still something that may need to be done, but it can still be done without negative words. Pray for the grace to accomplish this.

Speak No Evil

"With it (our tongue) we bless our God and Father, and with it we curse men, who have been made in the similitude of God."
James 3:9

This should not be. The story last time about my sister and me in the car is a picture of this. All people are made in the image of God and because of that we ought to give them cordiality. The incident in the car could have been detrimental to our relationship. It was not, praise God, but we need to consider our words. That does not mean we don't ever correct others, but somewhere there is a balance. The best thing I can come up with is to seek the Lord and correct when He says to and refrain when He says refrain. He seems to say refrain a lot. Paul tells us to correct in humility, which is to do it gently in order to be an example to the other to bring them to the right place with God.[106]

---

106. 2 Timothy 2:25

Mom used to tell us, "You are always being watched by others." Either they are cheering for you, hoping you won't mess up, or they are waiting for you to fail so they can have another statistic of a hypocritical Christian. Pray that you do not fall into the temptation of blessing God but cursing man because it is an easy one to fall victim to. Strive to be one who speaks as Christ would desire and not as the world does. We are to be set apart because we are a royal priesthood, a holy nation, a special people to proclaim the praises of Him who called us out of darkness into His marvelous light.[107] Because of this role, we are called to a higher standard. We have left the base jesting, dirty talk, and revengeful words and thoughts. He has asked us to walk the high road. We are to live as Christ lived. When we call ourselves Christians we have put on the role of being an ambassador of Christ and with that we are portraying to the world who Christ is. We are saying we are His children, and whatever we say and do will tell the world and other Christian onlookers who our heavenly Father is and what we think of Him. So, what will our witness say? Do our words align with the character of Christ or do our actions align with the world, aka the devil? Are our words and actions from the Father of lights or the father of lies? Who will the world see when they look at us? Who will God see when He looks at us? Will it be His Son?

---

107. 1 Peter 2:9

APPLICATION:

It is time to do another self-check to see how we are living. We want God to see His Son when He looks at us. So, find that same friend from the last time and ask them how you are doing as far as walking and talking as Christ would. W.W.J.D (What would Jesus do?).

Humility in Alignment

"Who is wise and understanding among you?
Let him show by good conduct that his works
are done in the meekness of wisdom."
James 3:13

When I was a very little girl, my parents decided to teach us the lesson of the joy of giving in secret. Every once in a while, on a Sunday morning, we would get to church at a time when no one was in the halls, and we would place little gifts on a table under the mirror in the main foyer. Each gift had a name of a widow or widower on it. Then we would go to church, and no one knew it was us, not until after we moved. But it was always a joy to watch or hear about the older people getting their gifts. Often times such folks are overlooked and they need to feel special too. All of us were sworn to secrecy so as not to draw attention to ourselves and the great deed we had done, but rather to be the invisible hands of God to warm an old heart. It is a trait of the meek to not have to be recognized for what they do. I, however, did not tell because

I enjoyed the idea of keeping the "big secret" and not because I was meek.

There is a "blessed" about meekness. "Blessed are the meek, for they shall inherit the earth."[108] When I think of meekness I think of humility. God loves a humble spirit. The works that we do ought to be done with a humble motive. If we do good works to show off, then Jesus said we do it to be seen by men, so we have received that as our reward.[109] However, when we do works out of obedience to the Father, and better still in secret, God will reward us openly.[110]

Why we do what we do needs to be because of Jesus. When a person is wise and has understanding, they must be extra cautious to exercise humility. I feel that those who grew up in a Christian home, like I did, have to work harder to be humble because we know the right answers and have been "good" our whole lives. It must be remembered that God detests the proud, but gives grace to the humble.[111] "A wise man conceals knowledge, but a man of understanding will draw it out."[112] Truly wise people don't go about proclaiming how wise they are. As others observe their words and actions, they gain the title of being a wise person. Or it may be that through their lack of wisdom, they obtain the sarcastic title of "wise guy." The way to gain wisdom is through the fear of the Lord, which

---

108. Matthew 5:5

109. Matthew 6:1-2

110. Matthew 6:3-4

111. 1 Peter 5:5

112. Proverbs 12:23

requires a measure of humility.[113] Don't look for wisdom in the loud showy places, but find it in the calm, consistent, faithful followers of God.

APPLICATION:

If you have not done this already, begin to practice thinking before you speak; this is a sign of wisdom. Ask questions before pronouncing assumptions, and ask in meekness, waiting to understand, not challenge. You want to be like Christ who asked questions.

---

113. Proverbs 9:10

The Watchman – When to Fight and When to Be at Peace

"But the wisdom that is from above is first pure, then peaceable, gentle, willing to yield, full of mercy and good fruits, without partiality and without hypocrisy."

James 3:17

Pick your battles. Wisdom won't fight everyone. My dad is good at this. When I have been frustrated and confused, I get feisty and Dad does two things really well. One is that he stays at peace and is gentle with me, which in turn calms me down. The other is if he is one percent wrong then he apologizes for the whole thing. Dad, in forfeiting his right to defend himself, is showing mercy to a weaker Christian. This is great wisdom.

These attributes remind me of the fruits of the Spirit: Love, joy, peace, patience, kindness, faithfulness, goodness, gentleness, and self-control.[114] How often do we see these fruits in our own lives? When opposition arises where is the mind? Is it ready to make a stand and fight back, like mine often is, or do we pause and become peaceable, gentle, willing to yield on non-fighting issues? You might think that if you are wise, you do not necessarily need to be peaceable or willing to yield. But a wise person knows that being peaceable can bring about a more harmonious outcome. A wise person also knows when their wisdom may not be appreciated and will do no good, and so they choose to be silent. I think we will be less likely to fight if we don't take an argument personally. In the past, when I have seen people behaving foolishly, I tried to correct them, and then got mad when they would not see the truth or wisdom that I offered. There are countless times when I gave unwanted advice just because I thought it might help and then the receiver of the counsel snapped at me because it was irritating more than helpful. Then I am either hurt or mad because they rebuffed my wisdom. According to James, though, I should have been full of mercy and probably stopped talking sooner. Ezekiel talks about the watchman whose job is simply to warn the people. If the watchman does not warn them, then their blood is on his head. However, if he warns them and they do not listen, then their blood will be on their own heads. The wisdom that is from above gives them the benefit of being warned and then the fruit of responsibility to choose.

Wisdom thinks before it speaks and acts, because it is pure and peaceable. Jesus is pure and peaceable, and we don't want to give a false picture of who He is, nor a poor representation

---

114. Galatians 5:22-24

of Him. We are to be His hands, His feet, and His mouthpiece. We want both our words and our actions to be in sync and ultimately to align with Christ. However, to align with Christ we must know Him, and the best way to do that is to spend time with Him and learn about Him through reading Scripture and listening to others who know Him. Most importantly, in order to gain the wisdom from above, we need to ask the One who is above, as the very first chapter of James says.

APPLICATION:

This is a difficult battle to fight in bringing our souls into alignment with His. You want your voice to be heard, but God's wisdom is to know when to be silent and turn the other cheek. Try not to get into word fights but ask God for discernment to know when your opinion is needed and when it does not matter. Ask for wisdom.

DAY THIRTY

Alignment in Our Prayers

"You ask and do not receive, because you ask amiss,
that you may spend it on your pleasures."
James 4:3

Remember the story about my family praying for jeans and God sent boxes of them? That was a time when we were truly praying for what we absolutely needed. Jeans were not for our pleasure, but were a necessity for working on the ranch. That prayer was not amiss. God does still give us pleasurable things, but when we pray it must be balanced with this verse. Recently, I was praying hard for someone. It was a time when I was repentant and I felt like I was at the altar before the Lord and could ask Him and He would be inclined to answer. Our world was turning upside down in many directions. My sister just went through the hardest correction of her life, and I was being asked to say goodbye to someone I really, really wanted to move forward with, not backwards. But as I prayed to God, I was asked if my intercession was for Him to give me back what I was going to give up or if it was for my sister. I chose to make it for my sister because I chose to believe that God asking me to give this man up was His will. Had I prayed that God would not make me give him up, it would have been amiss for my own pleasure and not trusting God with His will.

In verse two, right before this one, it said, "You do not have because you do not ask."[115] Do these verses contradict each other? No, they do not. God wants us to ask because He is willing and able to provide; He wants that relationship with us. However, the statement in verse two is balanced with verse three. God also tests the hearts and motives behind the request, and answers accordingly.[116] Because of that, He sometimes says no. If we are just asking to gain and advance our agenda and not to align ourselves with Him, why would He want to answer in the affirmative? He wants to bless us, but He also knows what is best for our eternal salvation. Aligning ourselves in prayer to His will is of the utmost importance. In that knowledge and wisdom He works on our hearts first. It is easier to work on a humble heart just as it is easier to mold clay when it is wet or to plant after the rain. Often in my life, I have been corrected and each time I either had the option to harden my heart and learn the hard way, or to open my heart for the rebuke so that I would not have to learn everything all over again. One particular time, my older sister corrected me on something (I don't remember what, because this happened all the time) and my first reaction was to be frustrated with her. So after correction, I typically go off alone and then God begins to work on my heart, shows me that I am wrong, that

---

115. James 4:2

116. Deuteronomy 8:2

she is right, and then I typically have a softer heart to learn what she is trying to teach me. It is not until I have a humble heart that I will actually be able to learn. When our hearts are proud, it makes our brains fussy and we cannot understand as well. If we were given all we wanted and asked for, few of us would remain humble and our hearts would not be moldable to God. We must want His will above all else, above the gifts He gives, above our own will and the desires of our heart, and we must trust His answers are for our best. We have faith and know that God can do all. Can we have faith that He will do what is best for us? When He gives His answer, will we be like David and worship even if it is not the answer we want, because God is good, sovereign and holy? David fasted and prayed for his child, yet God chose, in His wisdom, to take the life of the child as the punishment for David's adultery with Bathsheba. When David knew God had given His answer, he ate, washed his face, and went to the house of the Lord to worship.[117] Jesus said, Lord, I know you can do all things, please let this cup pass from Me; nevertheless, Your will be done.[118] He had faith and made a request. As we know, the answer to the prayer of the Beloved, Only Son, was a "no," and Jesus submitted to the will of God. The answer was not a "no" because Jesus prayed wrong or because Jesus wanted to consume His prayer on His own pleasure. It was a "no" because there was no other way to save the world. He died on the cross in total alignment and submission to the will of God. Our motives and our will need to be aligned with the Father's. How do we

---

117. 2 Samuel 12:20

118. Luke 22:42

do that? We ask what His will is; we listen; we watch for His word to be confirmed by two or three witnesses. We do not know because we do not ask. After we ask, we must obey. If we ask in accordance with His will, it will not be amiss. When we listen, God speaks. When we obey, God moves. When God moves, things happen.

APPLICATION:

Worship is perhaps your most powerful weapon along with prayer. This is because it drowns out the voice of our enemy. Your application is to worship and praise God when He says no. This can be done through listening to praise songs, singing, or even simply saying, "Praise God, praise God, praise God." That is what Mom used to make us do every time we said "ouch." Align with Christ by praising Him.

Christ Humbled Himself First

"But He gives more grace. Therefore He says: 'God resists
the proud, but gives grace to the humble.'"
James 4:6

When I was ten years old we had an Alabama red-and-white clay angel holding a baby. This was one of the few trinkets Mom loved and had displayed on the fireplace mantel. It was Christmas time and I was decorating and hanging lights all around the living room. I draped them over the mantel, and it looked beautiful. Unfortunately, I draped them around the angel and the weight of the colored lights brought the angel smashing onto the tiled floor. I did not stay to clean it up, but ran straight to Mom and told her I was sorry. By ten years of age I had learned to confess my mistakes quickly because it often made for a lesser punishment. Just as with the examples before, Mom also showed mercy. After ten years of searching, my sister and I finally found a replacement, not because we had to, but because we wanted to. When we gave the new angel to Mom for Mother's Day, she cried because we remembered.

Our verse is pretty straightforward, but let's dwell on the fact that God gives more grace to the humble like Mom did with me. He gives more grace even when we are so undeserving. We ought to endeavor to do the same. In this chapter James writes to remind us to humble ourselves in God's sight. [119]When King David sinned so greatly with Bathsheba he eventually humbled himself and wept over his sin. He fasted and prayed for mercy.[120] David knew that God would not reject a contrite and broken heart.[121] Through his repentance he wrote Psalm 51, humbling himself and aligning himself back under God. In the psalm he pleads with the Lord to create in him a clean heart and to renew a right spirit in him. He is asking to receive grace and come back into alignment with God. This gave him the right perspective when God chose to answer his petition for the life if his child with a no. When the son died, David accepted God's answer and worshiped.[122] David is rightly called a man after God's own heart. Even when wicked King Ahab humbled himself, God called him His servant.[123]

True humility is a beautiful and blessed attribute in God's sight and a rare occurrence in our society. Blessed are the poor in spirit and the meek, Jesus said. Theirs is the kingdom of

---

119. James 4:10

120. 2 Samuel 12:16

121. Psalm 51:17

122. 2 Samuel 12:20

123. 1 Kings 21:27-29

heaven.[124] In society a humble person is usually overrun and seen as unconfident and a pushover. In God's eyes, when we are humble we are seen as useful, glorifying, and moldable. Because we are trying, God gives us more grace to overcome our mistakes. Work at being humble not just before the Lord but throughout your life and interactions with others because it is desirable to God; it is one of His characteristics. We want to be pleasing to God and bear the image of His Son. Philippians 2:5-8 shows the perfect picture of humility when it describes Jesus. He was equal with God, yet He humbled Himself and became as a man, and then again as a man He still humbled Himself further to do the will of God. When we are humble we are moldable, and when we are moldable we are leadable by God. And where will He lead us? To the feet of Jesus. "The Lord is my light and my salvation; whom shall I fear? The Lord is the strength of my life; of whom shall I be afraid?"[125]

APPLICATION:

Take some time to locate three areas of pride in your life. Write them down and then repent. Pray for God to forgive you for having the despicable attitude of pride in your life and ask Him to teach you humility in each of the three areas. When you are tested in those areas, reach out to God and practice humility. Look for the areas of God's grace in your life and write them down and give God glory for them.

---

124. Matthew 5:3-5

125. Psalm 27:1

Alignment Only to God's Will

"Therefore submit to God. Resist the devil
and he will flee from you."
James 4:7

Now sometimes the temptation is to jump the gun and force something to happen before God's perfect time. When Abraham and Sarah did that, they got an Ishmael who now wars against the descendants of Isaac to this day. As I was writing this, I was working through the aftermath of jumping the gun. There was a guy who seemed to be exactly what I wanted in a husband, but God told me it was not His will. It took me three months to submit to God and an even longer aftermath of resisting the devil and reminding myself, "I do not want the devil's bread." When Jesus was tempted with food, He resisted the devil and chose to wait on God's timing. Look at the words Jesus used to rebut the temptation, "Man shall live by every word that proceeds from the mouth of God." Jesus was waiting for God to speak, not the devil. There was nothing wrong with bread, but the issue was that it was suggested by the devil and that it was not God's timing. When the temptations were complete, God then sent angels to attend to Him.[126] Part of our victory is in trusting and waiting on God's timing.

Because God gives grace to the humble, we ought to submit to Him, or in other words we should humble ourselves and bring our will under His. God's will is always best for us even when we don't see the good in it. Because we love and trust God, we choose to submit to His will and timing; however, while that sounds easy, we must not be deceived because it is harder than it sounds. We must resist the devil too. When we resist, expect push back, or a down-and-out fight, before the devil flees. Christ, while He was tempted in the wilderness, had to withstand and resist the devil many times before the devil left Him alone. Sometimes the temptation does not look wrong, but unlike Eve in the garden, we must trust and submit to the direction of God. Jesus was tempted to turn rocks into bread.[127] Could He have done it? Was His fast over? Could He have eaten? Was the action, in and of itself, bad? What mattered was not necessarily the action, but rather who was telling Him to do it. Don't eat the devil's bread!

By waiting on God we are trusting in His sovereignty. Submitting to God will help us overcome the temptations of the devil and the flesh, because when we submit to God we will be resisting the devil and he will leave us alone for a while.

---

126. Matthew 4:11

127. Matthew 4:2-4

APPLICATION:

When temptations come there is always a way of escape, a way to not give in to the desires of the flesh. Pray that God will show you the window and give you the courage to take it. Sometimes it requires reminding yourself out loud, "I don't want the devil's bread," to silence the enemy. When temptation arises, resolve in your heart now that you will submit to God, trust Him for a way out, and not give in to the flesh.

DAY THIRTY-THREE

Ever Close

"Draw near to God and He will draw near to you.
Cleanse your hands, you sinners; and purify your hearts,
you double-minded."
James 4:8

When I was in college I was struggling over my grades and God reminded me that He wanted my heart more than my grades. If on the judgment day I said, "But look at my grades," they would be burned up before Him because in eternity what matters is our relationship with Christ, not our accomplishments. As we are being purified, we must continue to choose Christ and His will above our own. There will be aspects of our lives we don't want to give up (like my worldly recognition in grades), but we must love Christ more than all else. If we don't, then we choose not to move closer to God.

When we seek God, He will be found. He is not far, nor is He hiding. If we reach out our hand, He will be there, just as He was for the woman with the issue of blood. She had been going to doctors for twelve years with no results. They were unable to stop her from constantly bleeding. But when she heard of Jesus she said to herself, "If I can only touch His clothes then I will be healed." And she was. The moment she touched Him, He turned to find her and tell her that her faith made her well.[128] Sometimes we have to ask for eyes to see, but He is always there. He says He will never leave us nor forsake us.[129] We are promised that as we come, so will He. Now God is holy and perfect so as we come to Him we must go through a process of purification; some call this sanctification. As we walk closer to God, He will show us things in our lives that need to be made right. When He tells us to change, we will be held responsible for our obedience or lack thereof. He calls us to clean our hands and purify our hearts, but how do we do this? By not being double-minded. This is the process by which we are transformed into His image. In order to stand before the Almighty and Holy God we must choose Him and be cleansed. Fire goes out from Him and consumes all wickedness,[130] and I don't want to be consumed and sent to hell. We ought to flee youthful lusts and run in the opposite direction, toward God. We walk with Christ through a cleansing process as He prepares us to meet His Holy Father. Being transformed is not easy. When the purification process happens we have to hang on to Christ for our strength because we don't have any. When we feel like it is too hard, we pray for strength and to be humble and moldable so we can be victorious by His grace. We must ask Him for the daily bread of His presence to

---

128. Luke 8:43-48

129. Hebrews 13:5

130. Psalm 97:3

get us through the day. That is never a prayer to be consumed on our own lusts. He will answer it. I know because that is what He has done for me. My family and I experienced three deaths in three years, a national pandemic, and struggles at home over my friend's rocky relationship. There were days I only got through by God's strength and His daily bread. "Taste and see that the Lord is good; blessed is the man who trusts in Him!"[131]

APPLICATION:

Aligning with Christ is sprouting from a desire to be close to Him. As you draw near you must be cleansed, so pray for His cleansing touch. Now this may come with fire, but don't be afraid for He is gentle. As He is cleansing you, you must make a conscious effort to submit to God and walk changed. May God send you His daily bread as you grow with Him.

---

131. Psalm 34:8

Alignment in the Beatitudes

"Humble yourselves in the sight of the Lord,
and He will lift you up."
James 4:10

I have a sister who has strived for a humble spirit. There came a time when she was having some trouble with keeping her attitude humble and I corrected her about her heart. She was humbled by the correction and allowed me to help her change to better please God. How she conducted herself after the correction (allowing others to pour in and change her for the better) is what it is to be humble.

So how do we humble ourselves in God's sight? I believe a key is in the prior verse when it says to mourn and weep, let your laughter be turned to mourning and your joy to gloom.[132] This is a mindset of grief over our sins. In Matthew it says blessed are the poor in spirit, … blessed are those who mourn, … blessed are the meek, … blessed are those who hunger and

---

132. James 4:9-10

thirst for righteousness for they have great reward.[133] When humbling ourselves we must be poor in spirit and realize our great need for Christ because of our inadequacy to overcome sin in our own strength. When we see our sin for the death that it is, we mourn and our joy is turned into gloom, but God encourages us that we are blessed because those who mourn will be comforted.[134] He comforts our hearts as He forgives us. After mourning we are being comforted; we are meek and moldable to Christ's touch, and that is when we hunger and thirst for righteousness, and we will be filled![135] As we draw near to God, humbling ourselves, He will both draw near to us and lift us up.[136] We need to be moldable by God through those godly examples He puts in our lives. Don't become obstinate and stiff-necked, which is our natural response; instead take the correction and allow it to change you for the better. We are not supposed to stay down in the muck and mire, but we are to be lifted up and made moldable by the Master's touch. Pure gold has been heated up and refined twenty-four times, and when it is pure it is fluid and moves easily to the jeweler's touch. Let us be beautiful pure gold for Christ. "He has made everything beautiful in its time."[137]

---

133. Matthew 5:3-12

134. Matthew 5:4

135. Matthew 5:6

136. James 4:8

137. Ecclesiastes 3:11

APPLICATION:

If you stay with God, even your hardships are made glorious. But in order to obtain that you must be responsive to your Master as He teaches you to bring your soul into submission to His. As you prove yourself faithful to His request, He will honor you to know more and more of Him. Pray to know Him.

DAY THIRTY-FIVE

Impacting the World

"Whereas you do not know what will happen tomorrow.
For what is your life? It is even a vapor that appears
for a little time and then vanishes away."
James 4:14

The past two years I have experienced loss and written so many sympathy cards, it all brings the hard reality screaming at me that my life here is limited and will end one day. This harsh reality does one of two things. One, it makes us want to cling to all we can get out of this world. Or two, it makes us see our frailty and ask how we can serve God in the short time we have here. We want to avoid being ready to die because we feel like it invites death, but we cannot afford not to be ready. This realization also teaches us humility and submission to the will of God because He is the One who numbers our days. If we only have a short time to make an impact for God in this world, shouldn't we be asking Him what He wants us to do with this life? The lesson from a headstone is that we only have a dash between two dates. That time fills a basket for the Lord that represents our life and what we filled it with. Therefore, as Paul says, let us redeem the times.[138]

What is our life? Scripture gives a clue that we live on this earth for seventy years, eighty if we are strong, but even in that we are not promised tomorrow.[139] Our life is a vapor. We spent so much time serving ourselves before we were saved, we ought to try all the harder to make up for lost time and use the rest of this vapor for Christ's work. We are not saved by works, but if each one of us is given a crown that represents our works for Him, and that we will cast at the Lord's feet, don't we want a crown full of jewels to give Him?[140] Everything created in this life is temporary except those things that bring spiritual profit.

If our life is a vapor, what will the fragrance of our vapor be? Will it be a repugnant smell to the Lord or will it be a sweet-smelling aroma that is pleasing to the Lord?[141] I had a professor who kept the perfume bottle his wife used at their wedding. Every now and again He pulls it out and smells it. When he does, it takes him right back to the best day of his life. We want to be a smell like that to God, one that brings Him inexplicable joy. Yet how we smell depends on how we respond to God and if we choose to humble ourselves in His sight and submit to Him or not. Pride is repugnant, but humility is sweet. The Holy Spirit wants to remain with people

138. Ephesians 5:16

139. Psalm 90:10

140. Revelation 4:9-10

141. 2 Corinthians 2:15

who give off a sweet-smelling aroma and He leads those who are humble and moldable.

APPLICATION:

Your time here is not yours, but God's, so ask Him what is one thing He wants you to do. Once you know, look for opportunities to practice it and have fruit for God. In doing this stay balanced and remember to only do what God asked you to do. When He says stay or asks you to not do something, hold still and don't do it just because it looks like a good opportunity. The sweet aroma you want comes from obeying. Seek and do.

Say, "If the Lord Wills"

"Instead you ought to say, 'If the Lord wills,
we shall live and do this or that.'"
James 4:15

One goat we had named Bordeaux hated medicine. To keep her healthy we would administer it as needed. It was our will, not hers. She would pretend to chew it and even swallow so we would think she obeyed. But as soon as we removed our hands, she would spit it out. Aren't we like that with God sometimes? We should not be. We ought to be submissive because even if His will is to give us awful tasting medicine, it is good for us. Perhaps sheep are more docile because sheep have poor eyesight and this knowledge makes them understand their dependency upon the shepherd. We don't know what the future holds and as humans we are very nearsighted, but too often we don't see this as a reason to humble ourselves and become dependent on the Shepherd. We behave like goats and do our own thing because we think we can see just fine and don't need a shepherd to be our constant guide. We think our best is to fake taking the medicine and then spit it out when (we think) God is not watching. Yeah right! We know He is always watching.

This verse implies a realization that God is sovereign. Nothing happens on earth without God knowing about it. Job is a prime example of this because the devil had to ask permission of God to touch Job and he also had to give an account to God of what he had been doing every time.[142] We can trust what God allows because of this truth. Nothing was allowed to touch Job without it going through the hands of a merciful God. It is the same with us. By saying "If the Lord wills..." we are reminding ourselves to align our will with His, and we are also reminding ourselves of His sovereignty over all that happens. Each day we should humbly surrender our will for His, and when things arise, we ought to check them with God first before jumping. Right before I began this study I was asked on a date and I did not pray about it and ask God if He wanted me to go. I simply set it up. The date itself was fine, but the aftermath was horrible, because I was wanting to pursue the relationship, but God closed the door. I had to surrender my will for God's will and that is not an easy process. So, when I complained to God, He showed me that I did not ask. I should have been shooting for God's will, not just having a good time with someone interested in me. We can plan our ways, but best check them with the One who knows and sees all first. A man plans his ways, but the Lord directs his steps.[143] It is good to have a plan, but always leave it open for God to direct and

---

142. Romans 14:12

143. Proverbs 16:9

change it. With this comes humility and submission. As we make choosing God's will and saying "If the Lord wills" a typical response in our lives, we will be able to stay on His path better. By doing this it gives us time to think before we act and ask God His opinion on the matter, thus keeping us aligned with Him. Placing our will under the will of God is essential to living a life that glorifies God, and because only Christ truly knows how to please God, He is our example.

The choice to plan your way and trust God's sovereignty is a simple one, but the daily living it out is a different story. When God's will happens, and not our plans, we have to die to self, give up our independence, our will, and rely on God. This is part of how to take up our cross daily, being ready to die to self so that Christ may live in us.[144] This sounds tough and slightly depressing, but the truth sometimes is. We will serve someone, either the devil or Christ. So why not serve the One who will love us, died for us, will always do what is best for us, and who is the Good Shepherd that leads us to eternal reward? The other, while perhaps seemingly more fun in this world, only comes to steal, kill, and destroy.[145] Choose Christ who brings eternal life, who said, "Not my will, but Yours, be done."[146]

APPLICATION:

The Bible tells us we are like sheep; we have spiritually bad eyesight. We can't see His plans. This should make us attentive

---

144. Matthew 16:24-26

145. John 10:10

146. Luke 22:42

and obedient to God, but too often we allow this uncertainty to give us an attitude with God. Stop! Humble yourself and ask God to teach you to be responsive to His call even if it means showing you how blind you really are. Also begin to practice saying "If the Lord wills." This will help you remember whose plans are supreme. Begin each day with surrendering your plans to Christ.

Disobedience = Directly Misaligned

"Therefore, to him who knows to do good
and does not do it, to him is it sin."
James 4:17

This book has taken the course of three years to write just because I have been busy with life, with a full-time job, and with a young adults' conference we do every year. Recently, God brought another man into my world. It sounds like this happens often, but it really does not. Just two in the last three years. This one actually made it past coffee. He was humble and kind and we lined up biblically on most everything. After ninety-nine days of "talking," God confirmed to me that I had to give him up. This was so much harder than just having the door closed by God. He confirmed this course through scripture passages I was studying for different Bible studies, going over this study, and my spiritual authorities. So, I said goodbye because I knew if I did not, I would be sinning.

This was one of the hardest things I have had to give up, but God always gives the strength to obey.

As your conscience will witness, knowing what to do and actually doing it are very different things. When we know God has told us what to do and we choose not to obey, we are willfully choosing to disobey the will of God. Hebrews tells us this is so wrong, so evil, that it is as if we crucified Christ again.[147] We have been studying and seeing that we are to put God's will above ours every time because we are servants of His. Here is where the rubber meets the road; are we just hearers of the word, or doers? Is our desire in God's goodness or our plans? When God calls us to do something hard, embarrassing, fun, or good, are we obedient or are we like a deceptive murky well that boasts about our clean relationship with Christ but does not have evidence of His truth in us? I can tell you from observation that those who boast about Christianity, but do not practice dying to self and obeying the will of God, are repugnant stains on the name of Christ. That should push us to try and bring God glory in all things, so hypocrisy does not turn people away from Christ. One of the times I knew God was asking me to pray over a woman, I blatantly refused because I was scared, like the servant who hid the one talent.[148] When my sister went up to the altar to pray over the woman, I then told God I was ready, but He did not let me go. He said, "No. I have sent someone else." That understanding of His disappointment was crushing. If we put God's known will above ours and the good work He desires, then we will truly love

---

147. Hebrews 6:6

148. Matthew 25:24-25

God and obey Him.[149] If we don't, we have willfully chosen to disobey, which makes us worse than the non-believer because we know better. Jesus said, if you love Me you will obey Me.[150] So can we say, if we disobey Him we do not love God? Do I obey every time? No, but each time I sin and fail I must humble myself and repent. We are to constantly be pressing toward the goal of living for Christ, being transformed to His image, and pleasing Him. We should be like time, constantly moving forward, never going back, but relentlessly moving closer and closer to God. We are not to be conformed to the lusts of this world but be transformed by the renewing of our minds, constantly bringing our thoughts to Christ. Our thoughts should line up with Philippians 4:8 so that we think on: whatsoever is true, noble, just, pure, lovely, of good report, virtuous, and praiseworthy. We will be transformed as we focus and practice putting God's will above our own and doing what He has asked us to do. Don't put it off—that is delayed obedience, not to mention it just gets harder the longer we wait to obey. If we are not doing what we know and has been confirmed is the will of God, then we are sinning. Be quick! Be humble. Repent and return to a merciful God.

APPLICATION:

Are you getting tired of all this refining? I know, me too, but we are not there yet. Our souls are not yet in the image of God. He will give us a reprieve, but like time, we must go on.

---

149. James 1:22-25

150. John 14:15

Paul says, "I will keep running the race, I press on."[151] Pray for endurance to keep on going with Christ. This is not a temporary change; this is a lifestyle.

---

151. Philippians 3:13-14

Living for Pleasure or Alignment

"You have lived on the earth in pleasure and luxury;
you have fattened your hearts as in a day of slaughter."
James 5:5

This passage reminds me of the parable of Lazarus and the rich man. The rich man indulged his flesh and never regarded Lazarus as an opportunity to serve God. He fed his desires and never really looked at what God had right in front of him. Lazarus was a starving beggar right outside the rich man's gates. They both died on the same day, one in luxury and the other in agony. When they reached the afterlife, Lazarus was in the arms of Abraham being comforted while the rich man was in fire and torment. When the rich man cried our and asked Abraham to allow Lazarus dip his finger in water to cool his tongue, Abraham said no. Abraham reminded the rich man that he had lived in luxury and Lazarus did not, so now he was in pain and Lazarus was at rest.[152]

Peter and Paul both encourage us to flee youthful lusts. Are pleasure and luxury lusts? They are certainly something that takes our eyes and puts them on ourselves and our worldly desires. If we are not watchful, these worldly riches will strangle us like the seed sown among the thorns.[153] Beware of the thorns, they do not help us redeem the times.[154] How much time have we wasted not serving God? Redeeming the times is understanding that the Lord will return soon and we want to make up for lost time when we were not serving God. If we continue to fatten our spirits on earthly pleasures, how are we redeeming the times? When we get so wrapped up in ourselves and our plans, we fail to live in submission to God's will. James tells the unsubmissive to weep and howl and mourn, because they lived a life to please themselves and not for the will of God. We must never get so wrapped up in ourselves and our life here that we don't take the time to be still and ask God what He wants for our lives. He has created each one of us for a purpose, but we will never find it if we are living for ourselves. However, when we surrender our all, and live for Christ, not only will we find our purpose, but we have faith and hope that we will fulfill it. When I finally surrendered my will for God's in 2016, He began to do wonders in my heart and taught me so I could write my first book, *First and Forever*. However, my surrender was tested again. Each time

---

152. Luke 16:26

153. Matthew 13:22

154. Ephesians 5:16

and each area of my life is brought before me and He asks if I will choose to continually surrender all and give up my desires to choose Christ.

APPLICATION:

Begin your prayers by surrendering your will and ask God to send and confirm opportunities to redeem the times. This can be in acts of service, words of encouragement, touching someone, giving a gift, or something else. Whatever it is, follow God's lead and guidance. Live life in surrender and submission.

Staying Aligned in the Pruning

"Therefore be patient, brethren, until the coming
of the Lord. See how the farmer waits for
the precious fruit of the earth, waiting patiently
for it until it receives the early and latter rain."
James 5:7

D ad buys flowers for my birthday. Often, he gives me a
rose bush instead of cut flowers. This year God has been
teaching me valuable lessons through my roses. I trimmed my
deep pink rose bush that I had received a few years ago and
potted the clippings. The trimmings were watered diligently,
and the pruning was constant. Every time a bud would grow, I
would snap it off, because the rose needed to establish its root
system before it could give its energy to providing flowers.
During that time of my life, I felt very much like the little roses: a relationship was popped off, the conference we host was
canceled, a pandemic happened, our Bible study was split, and
a nephew died. I felt very much pruned. I could not understand why God was pruning off the very flowers I was made

to grow. Yet, He was calling me to establish my root system in Him before I was to grow more flowers. I must be patient until He decides when it is time to bloom for Him again. Will God's people trust Him enough to wait on Him to fulfill what He said His will is? As we wait on God, He strengthens us for the path ahead and prepares our hearts to accept His will. He gives us daily bread to strengthen us each day. Let patience have its perfect work that we may be complete, lacking nothing.[155] Isaiah said wait upon the Lord and He will strengthen our hearts.[156] Jesus Himself said, "Let not your heart be troubled; you believe in God, believe also in Me."[157]

Jesus often used the example of the fig tree to show us how we needed to grow fruit, and that a tree will be known by its fruit. We ought to desire to see fruit in our lives, but fruit does not grow overnight. It grows when the farmer actively takes care of the tree so it will be strong enough to have fruit. We had two apple trees growing side by side. One year they were so loaded down with fruit that one of the trees actually snapped in half because it was not strong enough to bear the weight of the fruit. Mom trimmed those trees back so hard we had to wait three years before they had fruit again. We almost gave up hope that they would ever have apples again because the wait was so long. Most change takes time, and part of the test is to see if we will wait and be diligent when we see nothing coming from our work.

---

155. James 1:4

156. Isaiah 40:31

157. John 14:1

APPLICATION:

Much of alignment with God may feel like a pruning process, but be of good cheer; your roots are growing and you will grow too. Hebrews says, whom the Lord loves He corrects; because of that you are legitimized as His child.[158] Pray for strength to trust Him, and ask for confirmation of your growth.

158. Hebrews 12:6-11

Set Your Heart

"You also be patient. Establish your hearts,
for the coming of the Lord is at hand."
James 5:8

Growing up in our home, Dad used to say the table was not set until the salt and pepper were on the table. Salt and pepper were the last things on the table. Drinks were filled, food was on, and then the salt. Then we all sat down, but supper did not begin until everyone had been seated. We had to wait to eat until then and prayers were said, which is hard when you are young because it smells so good. Likewise, we are to be patient and in our patience we are to have our hearts set so that when the trumpet sounds we will be ready to fellowship with Christ.

Establish your hearts, make them ready, confirm them. Like Jeremiah was told to "set" his face like flint, set your heart as flint until the Lord Jesus comes. To "set" something is to have it in position and ready for presentation. Having a ring "set" is having the gem at the perfect place where it will be sturdy and most attractive. Or like setting the table for supper, as I mentioned above, is having it ready to receive the food and guests. Having everything ready, so when we are called to come eat, nothing is held up, and the fellowship begins. If we are set, when hard times come we will not be moved. Are we ready to hold fast to God, to rest in Him because our hearts are established in Him? How do we set our hearts and prepare them to withstand the wait? We ask the Lord for His strength and then we determine within ourselves that the truth will not be taken from us. Fall in love with God as well because when you are in love, you will wait. We work out our faith through fear and trembling,[159] study His word to show ourselves approved, ask godly, fruitful Christians who have gone before us for wisdom and counsel. Just as the table is continuously reset and the ring is rechecked so the jewel is not lost, we ask the Holy Spirit for the same, that He will help us by rechecking while we are establishing our hearts. We want and need guidance, and the most important asset to gain is wisdom and strength from God.

APPLICATION:

Be ready and set, so you can go and do for Christ. You are "on call" for good works. To be of the best use as God's hands and feet you need to be in alignment with Christ. Like a diamond ring, are you at the place that displays God to the best advantage to the world? What do you need to move in your life so you will fit the setting God has designed for you? Pray and ask the Lord to show you. Begin responding to what He says to do and be in alignment. You may want that accountability partner again for support.

---

159. Philippians 2:12

Praise Instead of Grumbling

"Do not grumble against one another, brethren, lest you be condemned. Behold the Judge is standing at the door!"
James 5:9

With everything that went on during 2020 and everything else that has happened with unresolved issues, I kind of got into the habit of complaining against those who hurt my family and me. When I grumbled it never helped me come to peace about any of the situations. Finally, the Lord was tired of my grumbling, much like with the children of Israel, and God sent a punishment that hit my family and me like a ton of bricks. I described it as being shot with a gatling gun. A close friend of ours saw my failure and exposed my grumbling to us in a very painful way. I am not going to describe it for the protection of that friend whom we have forgiven, but you all know what it feels like to have someone close to you painfully expose your weaknesses. That is what it was like. The next week was spent in repentance and mourning over the years of grumbling that I had fallen into. God has such patience with us and is merciful, but He loves us so much that He will not allow us to continue in sin for forever. Because of this we need to make sure that we keep ourselves clean with God and with others as much as possible. That week of repentance was literally spent apologizing to those whom I complained to and to those I complained about. Talk about some humble pie.

We do not know the day or the hour of the Lord's coming[160] which is why we must always have our hearts set on Him. We want, when He comes, to be found approved by God. One way to prepare ourselves is to always give thanks. Giving thanks does two things for our mindset. One, it takes our mind off the current and the temporary and places it on Christ and the eternal. Two, it aligns our thinking with the will of God because He is whom we are praising. So if praising aligns us with Christ, grumbling does the opposite and disconnects us from Christ. God does not take pleasure in complainers. Remember how He destroyed the people of Israel when they complained against Him about the manna from heaven? He sent quail and made them all sick.[161] We will have to give an account for every idle word we say;[162] how much more those said in grumbling and disapproval of God's sovereignty. We must trust that His will is always best. In that, there will always be something to praise and give thanks for. When I was in Bible study our words were explained as an aroma. When we complain it sends a stench to God's nose. But praise is a sweet aroma of sacrifice to God. When the Romans conquered a

---

160. Mark 13:32

161. Exodus 16:8

162. Matthew 12:36

people they burned incense which, to them, was a smell of victory. Our grumbling and complaining is a stench to Him. When we conquer the flesh with praise instead, we give God the scent of victory. Are you breathing? Then praise. Is God still on the throne? Then praise! Are His mercies new every morning? Then praise! Find reasons to praise when you feel like grumbling or complaining.

APPLICATION:

For every difficult situation you come across, find three things to praise God for. Focus on these and say them out loud. Keep telling yourself these truths until you release the stress that was causing the urge to grumble is gone. It is a change of focus. Or you can write down 1000 things to be thankful for.

Enduring with Patience to Keep Aligned

"Indeed we count them blessed who endure. You have heard of the perseverance of Job and seen the end intended by the Lord – that the Lord is very compassionate and merciful."
James 5:11

There was a woman who was married with twelve children and one day her husband just left. She struggled for seven years to keep her family afloat. Every day she prayed for her husband, and every day when he did not come home she trusted in the Lord anyway. After seven very hard years God reunited them and because of the wait, God's glory through her testimony is all the more powerful. Through trials we learn to trust and wait on God, and to ask for patience.

There once was a man named Job. This man was righteous before God and the devil hated him. One day the devil asked permission to take everything away from Job to prove that Job's love was only based on what God could give him. After Job passed that test and remained righteous before God, the devil obtained the power to physically torture Job. In all of this loss of his possessions, his children, and his health, he would not let go of the trust he had in God, even though Job could not see the end of his trials.[163] Very rarely can we see the end that the Lord has in mind, yet we know Him to be a good, gracious, and loving Father who does what is best for us. Because of who God is, we can endure the trials. James says, in the very beginning of his letter, to rejoice when we have trials because they teach patience.[164] We are to endure, trusting God to make it right in the end. When God has walked us through we can look back and say, "God is good, and I have never seen the righteous forsaken."[165] Patience is not something I pray for, but I need it. Hastiness is a sin and being still is a rare gift.[166] James teaches patience to draw us closer to Christ, in order that we might know His will and be transformed into the image of Christ.[167] When we have endured, we will be given a crown of life.[168] So will we wait on God and trust in Him through trials like Job did? Remember, "Seek first the kingdom of God and His righteousness, and all these things shall be added to you."[169]

---

163. Job 1:8-22

164. James 1:2-3

165. Psalm 37:25

166. Proverbs 19:2

167. 2 Corinthians 3:18

168. James 1:12

169. Matthew 6:33

APPLICATION:

Will you trust in God enough to wait on Him? Trust that whatever it is that you are waiting for, God will do what is best. It may not be what you want or expect, but in the long haul, it will be best. When you wait on God and trust Him for what is best, you will grow in your relationship with Him and be fulfilled. So today, ask God to give you some piece of wisdom to help you in the waiting.

DAY FORTY-THREE

Walking in a Manner of Integrity

"Now above all, my brethren, do not swear, either by heaven or by earth or with any other oath. But let your 'Yes' be 'Yes' and your 'No,' 'No,' lest you fall into judgment."
James 5:12

I learned about letting my "yes" be "yes" at age eighteen. When I was young I always had an allergy to sugar. It made me have trouble breathing and caused black rings to appear under my eyes, so much so, my sister thought I had been punched. Mom tried all kinds of diets and the best one was to avoid processed sugars, but it did not stick. So when I was eighteen, my future brother-in-law was telling us how he had quit sugar. I was out praying that night and I knew the no sugar diet was the one that worked the best, so I told God I would only have sugar once a week. But I knew that if I told God I would do something, I had to keep my word. Possibly, the only reason this "diet" stuck was because of fear of the Lord and letting my "yes" be "yes". Since then, I have had one sugar day a week.

We do not want to do anything that would discredit who God is and the honor due His name. Back in Bible days people would swear by things greater than themselves in order to prove their sincerity.[170] But God calls us to a higher standard. We don't have to prove our honesty by swearing. Because of our respect for the Lord, we ought to let our word be true. If we are people of our word, we don't need to swear at all because we are people of integrity and others will learn that about us.

We don't want to give the enemies of God any reason to reproach the Lord because of us. When David sinned with Bathsheba, God reprimanded David for giving the other nations cause to discredit God.[171] Let us not allow our words to dishonor or discredit Jehovah. We should think before we speak, knowing we will be held by what we say. James also tells us to be quick to hear, slow to speak and slower to anger.[172] I need to work on this, because I find myself too often getting spun up over the slightest changes to my plans. When people see us, we want them to see a reflection of Christ, someone who is always true to their word and who doesn't get angry at the drop of a hat. Realize that our words have power and we ought to be careful of what we say. We need to act and speak as ones who have been changed by Christ from the inside out. When Christ changes us on the inside where no one can see, it displays itself on the outside for the world to see, and to give glory to God.

---

170. Matthew 23:16-22

171. 2 Samuel 12:14

172. James 1:19

APPLICATION:

Practice watching your words. Every time you have the urge to explode, swear, or add adjectives to defend yourself, stop. It is not needed. In the excess of words, sin is not lacking.[173] If you hold yourself accountable and by your actions prove yourself to be an individual of integrity, others will know that when you give your word, it is as good as done. Hopefully, they will also know that you do this because of Christ.

---

173. Proverbs 10:19

Align a Suffering Spirit

"Is anyone among you suffering? Let him pray. Is anyone among you cheerful? Let him sing psalms."

James 5:13

In 2020 and 2021 I got to experience the hardship of a suffering spirit. Technically, I was physically healthy, but my spirit was in anguish as I watched a friend live a double life and I was torn on her behalf. I prayed and am praying hard that she will come back and live one life to God. To know where she came from and to see where she is headed breaks my heart and right now, I am blessed to live with it and learn whatever it is that God will teach me from this spiritual struggle. But I must remind myself that even though my heart aches to have her back on track, God wants her back more than I do. And He wants me to stay in alignment with Him. As I prayed for change, He began on me with no sign of answering as I asked. Even when it seems that our prayers are ineffective, keep praying because we want to be in alignment with Christ.

James 5:13 is teaching us how to respond to our circumstances in a way that aligns ourselves with Christ. When we are suffering and going through hardships we are called to pray. Often when going through trials we are inward focused but when we humble ourselves and pray as we are meant to, asking God for His will, we are aligning ourselves with Christ. This is a very essential place to be for a child of God. Praying seems to begin its work on the one who is humble. So, we humble ourselves and submit ourselves to God's will and pray.

When we pray in these times of suffering we remember that these times are meant to shape us, mold us, and transform us into the image of Christ. So we ought to always be praying for God's will to be done, not simply that we will get out of the hardship. As we go through fiery days and we are being shaped, it may feel like we are being punished, but Hebrews tells us we are legitimized when God corrects us, because He loves us.[174] Pray instead for victory. And when we are cheerful, we sing praises to His name. This again aligns us with Christ because when we are feeling good we need to remember the One responsible for the good days, lest we think it is of our own doing or someone else's, or the result of chance. So, we sing to God, thanking Him for where we are. All that we do ought to be in the will of God. James is trying to teach us how to keep our focus on Christ in the times of affliction and in the times of plenty. We can be like Paul and be content in every season.[175]

---

174. Hebrews 12:6-8

175. Philippians 4:11

APPLICATION:

Know that your first priority is the relationship between you and God. When you are involved in a difficult situation that you are praying about, He will work on you first. So when He does, your application is to praise Him that He has found you worthy to be worked on by His hands. Your goal is to hear Him say, "Well done, good and faithful servant."[176] So ask Him if there is anything standing in the way of Him saying that today. May God touch your heart so you will know what it is He wants you to work on, and may He keep the enemy away so the seed will fall on good ground.[177]

176. Matthew 25:21

177. Mark 4:8

DAY FORTY-FIVE

Choosing to Be Submitted

"And the prayer of faith will save the sick, and the Lord will raise him up. And if he has committed sin, he will be forgiven."
James 5:15

In August of 2019 my beloved grandmother was diagnosed with lung and brain cancer, and given six months to live. While our will would have been to keep her here forever, that was not God's plan. After praying about it, we all collectively felt that her diagnosis was God's will. So we accepted the will of the Almighty, and instead of praying for healing for her, we prayed for strength for my grandfather who loved her for over sixty-four years. Acceptance is not always easy or fun, but it is right and God-honoring.

God hears the prayers of the righteous,[178] and does not reject those who have a contrite heart and a broken spirit.[179] We must remember to be praying God's will. Christ modeled

---

178. Proverbs 15:29

179. Psalm 51:17

this for us in the Lord's Prayer. He said, "Your kingdom come and Your will be done."[180] We are here to advance God's kingdom and to do His will. However, how often do we really want God's will above our own? Too often I find myself wanting God's will to be my will, not my will to become His. This is critical honesty and with the Holy Spirit's help will lead to repentance and humility. We must be at the place where we desire God's will above all else, as Jesus did in the garden where He wept bitterly but chose to submit Himself to the will of God.[181] When we submit to the will of God we become moldable, and that is when God changes us and uses us. It may not be the answer our flesh wants, but His answers are best for us, and if we are seeking His will, we will receive His response with acceptance. When we accept and do not fight the will of God, He is pleased and willing to use us. Acceptance also allows Him to comfort us as He wants to. King David begged God for his son's life, but when God chose to take his son, David worshiped even though the answer was radically different from what he prayed for.[182] Jesus submitted to the will of God even to the death on the cross.[183] Jesus is our example of how to live. The prayer of a righteous man will be heard. God does hear and He does answer.

APPLICATION:

Pray and ask God for His will and for our hearts to desire it.

---

180. Matthew 6:10

181. Luke 22:41

182. 2 Samuel 12:20

183. Philippians 2:5-8

Alignment Without Change Is Disobedience

"Confess your trespasses to one another, and pray for one another, that you may be healed. The effective fervent prayer of a righteous man avails much."

James 5:16

There is a man I know who went to the elders of the church, took them this verse and asked for healing. So, the elders gathered around him and before they prayed for healing they confessed their own sins to each other so there would be nothing between their request to God and the healing. How humbling. The man was indeed healed, but how many of us want God to move so much that we literally confess our hidden, inward sin out loud to another person? Would we dare to do that?

As we move into alignment with God, we begin examining ourselves, and when the Holy Spirit moves in us and we find sin and iniquity in our lives, we ought to confess it and repent.

Now, when I think of the word *fervent* I think of active dedication like commitment to pray about a specific issue until it happens. Sometimes God wants us to pray about something for a long while. Either it can be to test us so He sees how great our desire is or maybe it is to test how long we will trust without receiving an answer, or to have us wait so we will be ready for His answer. One time God had me wait so that I would be so hungry for an answer, that I would be inclined to obey. I wanted to do something for Him so I would not feel like I was wasting my life. There were about three months of feeling like a dog on a leash waiting to be released. Eventually, God placed me in a pregnancy center to minister to expectant moms. Those days that summer grew my faith so much. I got to watch a co-volunteer with her new Christian fire that made me question why my fire was not as bright. I got to hear the prayers of the women around me which strengthened my ability to pray in public. So that summer was necessary for my spiritual growth. When God causes us to wait, maybe something else is going on that we don't even understand and that is why He has not answered. Daniel prayed and fasted twenty-one days before he received an answer to prayer, but it was not because God did not respond. Gabriel said, "I was dispatched immediately, but I was detained in spiritual warfare."[184] Will we give up because we don't see an immediate answer from God? If so, what is our faith based on? If we have faith in the goodness of God, will we not wait on His response? My neighbor's mother waited and prayed for seven years for God to answer her prayers to bring her husband home. When other women with

---

184. Daniel 10:12

wandering husbands came to her and asked how long do you wait, she would say, "At least seven years." How long will we wait for God without ceasing to pray and without an answer?

APPLICATION:

I challenge you to continue to pray even when you feel that nothing is happening. The idea of a "wasted" prayer is one of the devil's tricks to stop the war that is raging in the spiritual world. There is no such thing as wasted time before God. You can't see the impact your prayers have on that battlefield. So, pray in faith that God has heard and be patient in that faith.

God Answers the Prayers of Normal People

"Elijah was a man with a nature like ours, and he prayed earnestly that it would not rain; and it did not rain on the land for three years and six months."
James 5:17

This is not what I normally think of when I think "answered prayers." However, Elijah was praying God's will so that the word of God would be fulfilled and the people of God would know He lives. This gives me hope that God listens to the prayers of "normal" people, those who were not perfect, who messed up and tried again. It is okay to pray hard things (in the will of God). David prayed that the Lord devour his enemies.[185] He also prayed for God to search his heart and test him that he would be found holy.[186] How many of us would ask the Lord to test us? Do we really want to know how bad we

---

185. Psalm 109

186. Psalm 139:23

are? We ought to learn what pleases God and pray for it. This is hard for me to do because I want what I want so badly. But this life is about more than being blessed on this earth. When I was little, Mom used to remind me that I was born to serve God. Jesus said to love Him with all that we are. How do we do that if we are not praying for His will? We know from the book of James that God answers prayers; we just need to pray without doubting and not to consume it on our own lusts.[187] Why do we struggle with this? Perhaps it is because we still have not humbled ourselves and given all to God. It is difficult to give the things we love the most to God. But there are no hands more capable than His. And it makes us ask how much we really love Him. He is what we are to love the most. As we align with God we will learn to trust Him more with things that matter. When I hold something more dear than Christ, He gently reminds me that it is an idol in my life, and He must pry it out of my hands. As we submit to God and draw near to Him, seeking His heart, He will teach us how to pray.[188] We have but to ask. He is good and is willing and ready to answer our prayers.

APPLICATION:

Ask God to teach you how to pray, just as His disciples did.

---

187. James 4:2-3

188. Luke 11:1

DAY FORTY-EIGHT

Get Back Up

"Let him know that he who turns a sinner from the error of his
way will save a soul from death and cover a multitude of sins."
James 5:20

One day we were doing a home Bible study with some
ladies and my sister washed all our feet. For everyone,
she had something to say that she believed God put on her
heart. But when she got to me, He wanted to talk with me
Himself, so He gave her nothing. What He told me was, "In
this Christian life, you will get dirty from running, but come
to Me and I will wash you." Whenever our feet become muddy
from this Christian life, make sure to see it and come to Christ
to be washed so we can get up and get back out there.

God is the One who saves; however, we get to be the hands
and feet of Christ, the instrument He uses. When God brings
a sinner back, He washes them clean again. When we walk
out of the hands of God, we walk right into a pig pen and get
dirty with our sin and our iniquity, so when we come back
He has to wash us all over again. Similarly, the father with the

prodigal son embraced his long-lost son and gave him clean clothes to wear.[189] This son may not have been with the pigs immediately after leaving his father's house, but his actions certainly led him there. Whenever we move toward God in humility and meekness, He runs to us and closes the gap, just like the father did. God makes up the difference. It is a matter of turning the prodigals back, to repoint them in the right direction with truth.

The truth will not always be accepted, so don't be surprised or hurt when it is not appreciated by others. Simply follow the Lord's lead for when to speak and when not to, for He knows what is going on in their hearts and yours. When the truth that we give is rebuffed, realize that sometimes all we can do is love them. But Christ knows the balance of when to say something and when to say nothing. As we fight to stay aligned with Him, He will tell us in each situation what to do, and will give us the strength to obey.

Remember, in all things walk humbly before the Lord. We want to follow God's lead unless we wander from His truth because we have pushed out on our own like the prodigal. May God grant us the strength, endurance, and grace to align with the One who is Truth, who knows all, sees all, and is compassionate. When we run back to the Father in humility and repentance, not only does a soul get saved, but God covers a multitude of sins as well because He is so gracious. "The Lord is good to all, and His tender mercies are over all His works."[190]

---

189. Luke 15:20

190. Psalm 145:9

APPLICATION:

Now go, walk in alignment with Christ and fight for your soul. As you are going teach others to do the same, that we all may be aligned with our Savior.

There Is a Battle for Our Souls, Which Side Are You On?

James has taught us many lessons regarding how to fight for our souls. Our soul is a very sought-after creation that finds itself in the middle of a war. One side calls out in gentleness, wanting us to choose the life Christ died to give us. The other side yells and pulls to force us to come be with everyone else on the highway to hell. James teaches that contrary to the world, we will win with Christ through humility, submission, and obedience to the will of God. The trials that we go through are evidence that we are in a war. Be encouraged as trials come our way because that means Christ is training us to fight better. Funny thing is, to win the war, we must surrender. Let me encourage you to everyday choose to hear and obey the voice of God, being doers of the word and not hearers only. May this book direct you to see the battle differently, allow yourself to be refined by God, and trust Him more as you align with Him.

Thank you for walking through this journey with me. Remember what God has taught you and live it.